CW00481044

LAWMEN
OF THE WILD WEST

For my wife Wendy with thanks for her forbearance and help with the editing and reading of this and other books.

LAWMEN
OF THE WILD WEST

TERRY C. TREADWELL

FRONTLINE
BOOKS

LAWMEN OF THE WILD WEST

First published in Great Britain in 2021 by

Frontline Books
An imprint of
Pen & Sword Books Ltd
Yorkshire - Philadelphia

ISBN 978 1 52678 233 5

A CIP catalogue record for this book is
available from the British Library

Typeset in 10.5/13 pt Palatino
by SJmagic DESIGN SERVICES, India.

Printed and bound by CPI Group (UK) Ltd, Croydon, CR0 4YY

Pen & Sword Books Ltd incorporates the Imprints of Aviation, Atlas
Family History, Fiction, Maritime, Military, Discovery, Politics, History
Archaeology, Select, Wharncliffe Local History, Wharncliffe True Crime
Military Classics, Wharncliffe Transport, Leo Cooper, The Praetorian Press
Remember When, Seaforth Publishing and Frontline Publishing.

For a complete list of Pen & Sword titles please contact

PEN & SWORD BOOKS LTD
47 Church Street, Barnsley, South Yorkshire, S70 2AS, England
E-mail: enquiries@pen-and-sword.co.uk
Website: www.pen-and-sword.co.uk

Or

PEN AND SWORD BOOKS
1950 Lawrence Rd, Havertown, PA 19083, USA
E-mail: Uspen-and-sword@casematepublishers.com
Website: www.penandswordbooks.com

Contents

Introduction

There were a number of different levels of lawman in the early years of the development of the American territories, and it might be helpful to briefly explain the differences between their powers of jurisdiction.

There were the town marshals, city marshals and constables who were employed by the local townspeople and whose authority was restricted to within the town or city limits. Then there were the county sheriffs who were elected by the citizens of the county, to keep the peace within the county. There were Texas Rangers and Arizona Rangers, who operated under the jurisdiction of their respective state governors. The United States Marshals, however, were appointed by the President of the United States, and had the authority to operate anywhere in

Right: Constable's badge.

Below: Arizona Rangers.

A collage of lawmen's badges.

the United States of America and deal with federal crime. Each of these law enforcement officers employed their own deputies, all of whom had the same powers of enforcement.

There was a school of thought that said that the most effective lawmen were once criminals, and they were not all pillars of society; although a large number were. Their job was, without a shadow of doubt, one of the hardest and most dangerous jobs in the West. In some cases notorious gunfighters were employed as town marshals to help bring law and order to some of the most lawless of towns. Television and movies covering the western era have highlighted the role of the sheriff, but have also been less than factual. The number of times the local town marshal has been seen to ride out of town to arrest a suspect is too numerous to mention. This was a myth, as the town marshal's powers were confined to the town itself, unless of course he was also a deputy sheriff with authority to make an arrest outside the town limits. In some of the larger towns the town marshal and the county sheriff had separate offices in the same town, and in these cases the sheriff could make the arrest, but both parties operated independently of each other.

The requirements needed to be a peace officer at the time were usually determined only by the individual's skill with a gun, and their courage. At times judgement was needed with only seconds to determine it, and that also meant that there was the odd occasion when justice and law never quite meant the same thing. The expression 'justice without law' was never truer than in the formative years of the West.

It was in this environment that the peace officer attempted to do his job, and many gave their lives trying to bring a semblance of law and order to the towns, cities and states that made up the United States of America. When the Congress of the United States created the Supreme Court and the Federal Justice system under the Judiciary Act of 1789, they also created the office of US Marshal.

The office of marshal can be traced back to the 14–15th century when they were known as *Mareschals,* or 'keepers of the horse', for the Teutonic war chiefs in Germany. Derived from two Gothic words, *Marah* meaning horse and *Calc* meaning servant, they soon became morphed into one – *Mareschal*. Over the centuries the status of the position increased and the title began to be applied to various important roles. In England in the 17th century, the position of *Mareschal du Banc du Roy* (Marshal of the King's Bench) was created. Among the *Mareschal*'s many duties was the keeping of law and order in the court of the king. This title was still active right up until the late 19th century. With the development of the colonies in the 'New World', the role of the *Mareschal* appeared once again, only this time it was known as the 'High Marshal' and it was his job to guard prisoners and maintain discipline in the courts. In the 1600s the office and title of Sheriff appeared in America and it began to take over the role of the High Marshal. Slowly the title of High Marshal disappeared, but in the southern states the title Colonial Marshal was retained right up until the War of Independence. The title of Sheriff comes from the old English word *scirgerefa* derived from *scir* (meaning shire, but now more commonly known as county) and *gerefa* (reeve or senior official).

In the early years of colonial America the only laws were those that were created by the churches or the elders of towns. The British, who still had some semblance of control, tried to impose the same laws they adhered to in Britain. The colonials, however, had different ideas, and as they moved away from the coastal towns and into the virgin territories beyond, they tended to ignore some of the 'British' laws and replace them with their own. The laws that may have applied in a civilised

Britain most certainly didn't apply in the wilderness of the Americas. Among the laws they tended to ignore were those that forbade trading guns and liquor with the Indians. The colonists decided only to obey the laws that did not interfere with their chance of surviving, making a profit, or with their consciences.

With lawlessness increasing, groups of vigilantes sprang up, and one of the first of these was the South Carolina Regulators, who operated between 1767 and 1769. They enforced the law in the territories where there were no courts or law, and although they usually kept within a semblance of the law, there was a propensity toward violence under the umbrella of justice.

In the larger cities that were springing up, the subject of law and order became a major issue with politicians, and steps were taken to safeguard the citizens by introducing night patrols of law enforcement officers. In New York this became known as the 'rattle watch', after the rattles carried by the officers to warn other officers if they were in trouble.

The need for law and order increased as the population expanded, and as the territories that needed policing got larger, more and more peace officers were required. Then, in 1789, the first of the US Marshals

South Carolina Regulators, the first organised body to try and maintain law and order.

appeared. In 1789 there were 15 districts with a marshal in each, by 1801 there were 22 states, and by 1850 there were 21 states and four enormous territories, each of the latter having three to four marshals.

In an effort to raise the status of the marshals and their deputies, Congress, in May 1792, passed a law stating that US Marshals had the same powers in each state, as those of the sheriffs in their districts. Some years later another law was passed that stated that although the federal marshals had to conform to common law, they were not required to conform to the duties of the sheriff. This in effect gave the marshals powers to enforce the law throughout their state, whereas the sheriff was confined to his district. The first US Marshal to be appointed was Robert Forsyth, and just five years after his appointment he became the first marshal to be killed. He was to be the first of over 400 Marshals to die in the line of duty over the next 200 years.

The US Marshals came under the control of the Secretary of State from 1789 to 1853, and after that they were passed to the office of the Attorney General. Control of the marshals was a mixed bag. The President of the United States, with the consent of the Senate, appointed them subject to a four-year term of office, which was renewable at the discretion of the new, or returning, President. Deputy US Marshals were appointed, and paid for, by the US Marshal in the district in which they served. In 1844, problems arose when some of the federal judges questioned whether or not the deputy marshals had any legal powers as officers of the court.

Deputy US
Marshal's badge.

They argued that the marshals, not the courts, employed the deputies, so the validity of their powers became questionable. The problem was resolved when the Attorney General at the time, John Nelson, ruled that when the deputies took their oath of office, it automatically made them officers of the court.

The marshals were paid by Congress but worked under the direction of federal judges and the courts. It is interesting to note how the role of the marshal changed over the years. One aspect of this is demonstrated by how, in the 19th century, it was a marshal's job to hunt down escaped slaves and return them to their owners, who then meted out their own punishment. Then, in the 20th century, it became his job to protect the slave's descendants from abuse of their civil rights and ensure their freedom.

The position of sheriff or town or city marshal at this time was confined to the towns and cities – he was the local policeman. This was another of those underpaid, thankless jobs that always seemed to arise in law and order, and required someone with more of a social conscience than a need to get rich.

The role of the marshal in these formative years was to support the federal courts that operated within the various judicial districts, and to carry out lawful orders issued by the federal judges within those districts. The job of the marshal and his deputies was an onerous one. Not only did they have to 'police' their districts, arresting criminals, serving warrants, writs and any other business decided on by the courts, but they had to be responsible for, and handle, all prisoners that were to be brought before the courts. In addition to this, it was the responsibility of the marshal that the courts functioned properly: they had to rent the courtrooms and gaol space, and employ bailiffs and cleaners. It was also their responsibility to pay the expenses incurred by the court staff, jurors, witnesses and even the US attorneys. They had to make sure the prisoners were presented to the court on time, that all the jurors and witnesses were present, and even make sure the water jugs in the courtroom were freshly filled. The ultimate task assigned to US Marshals and sheriffs was the execution of convicted prisoners.

This of course meant that the US Marshal had to work closely with the sheriff of either the county or the town in which he was operating. The duties of the marshal appeared to be more aligned to those of an accountant than of a peacekeeper. In Washington an army of accountants kept track of every cent spent by the marshals and would disallow anything they did not think was necessary. This of course raised the question of whether the people in Washington had any idea of what it

'Paddy' wagon used by Deputy US Marshals to transport prisoners.

was like to attempt to keep law and order in these vast, almost lawless territories, and keep control of a tight budget. The short answer is no! The town, district, or county over which they presided, on the other hand, paid sheriffs and so they did not have the same tight restrictions placed upon them as US Marshals. There were no fixed salaries for Deputy US Marshals: they were paid in the way of fees. He was paid six cents per mile while on official business, but all his expenses like food, board, ammunition and any sundry expenses had to be paid for by him up front. Receipts had to be obtained and this caused numerous problems, because obtaining receipts in the Indian Territory was almost impossible when the vast majority of the population could neither read nor write. When bringing a prisoner back it usually meant travelling for days, sometimes weeks, and all the expenses for this had to be paid for by the deputy marshal. He was allowed 10 cents per day to feed himself and his prisoner and pay for any assistance he might require. On submitting his claim for his expenses, the US Marshal took 35 percent of the total, leaving his deputy with just 65 percent. Judge Isaac Parker fought long and hard for his deputies to be paid a salary, saying that 'the service that these honest, trustworthy men gave was indispensable and if it wasn't for these men he would not be able to hold court for one single day'.

If all this sounds totally time-consuming and confusing, the marshal and his deputies also had the job of taking the national census every 10 years and collecting statistical information on manufacturing and commerce, together with numerous other tasks. Considering that there was usually only one US Marshal per state and possibly a handful of deputies, the area that had to be covered was vast, and it sometimes took days or weeks to bring prisoners into the nearest gaol or courthouse. This often meant travelling through hostile Indian Territory and being subjected to horrendous weather conditions. This was not a job for the faint-hearted, but one that required dedication, strength and fearlessness. In addition to this the Deputy US Marshal, when he arrested a suspect, had not only to make sure that he had committed an offence, but also bring to court witnesses and evidence to support the prosecution of the offender.

Public trust in the marshals at this time was shaky to say the least. Most of the colonists had come from Europe, predominantly from Britain, where they only recognised and trusted positions of authority that had arisen through tradition and custom. The role of sheriff was one that had existed in Britain since the seventh century, and so the position of sheriff in America was recognised by the colonists as one of authority.

What does become abundantly clear is that the number of constables, deputy sheriffs, sheriffs, town marshals, marshals and Deputy US Marshals that had criminal records, before and after becoming lawmen, was quite staggering. The saying 'You need to set a thief to catch a thief', was never truer. The job required someone who had experienced life on the other side of the law, to understand the mindset of those who now continued to break the law.

One of the major problems marshals had to deal with was the vigilante groups who meted out their own punishment to wrongdoers. Even the most trivial of crimes could be met with whippings or even hangings, depending on the whim of the people at the time. Lynch law was one of the biggest problems facing the marshals and sheriffs. This had come about after the collapse of the court system and the lawlessness that accompanied it.

After the American War of Independence (1775–1783), the population started to increase, which invariably meant that crime also increased

Sheriff looking at the body of a rustler who was lynched after being caught in the act.

and this called for more officers of the law. This also meant that more marshals had to be appointed. Selection in these formative years was restricted to nominations rather than experience. The vast majority of marshals did not stay in the job very long, as there was no training, and any skills that some had had in law enforcement usually came from having served at one time or another as sheriffs or deputy sheriffs. It was also considered to be a thankless task for small remuneration.

Furthermore, there were no professional lawmen around in these times. It was a job that was taken up like any other, and the person remained in the job until something better came along, or, it was decided by the townspeople that it was time for them to move on.

There were also problems in being a marshal and having to serve in a district where he had grown up and knew almost everybody. It was this local knowledge that caused some marshals to have a conflict of loyalties, as in the case of US Marshal John M. McCalla of Kentucky in 1832. He had been ordered by the courts to confiscate more than 10,000 acres of land belonging to 30 families who had lost their court case to keep the land. He felt that the families had been treated badly by the courts, because the vast majority of them were illiterate and totally ignorant of the law and had been unable to make a case for themselves. He wrote to the Attorney General, Roger B. Taney, stating this, but was told that it was not his place to take sides, but to do his duty as a federal US Marshal – which he duly did, albeit very reluctantly.

In 1846 the Mexican governor of New Mexico surrendered the territory to the American army led by General Stephen Watts Kearney. He appointed a local businessman from Santa Fe, Richard Dallam, as US Marshal for the territory. It was obvious that the area was too big to cover properly, so Chief Justice Joab Houghton divided it into three districts, each with its own headquarters. These headquarters were in the towns of Albuquerque, Santa Fe and Taos. But one year later the smouldering resentment towards the American army exploded into what was to be known as the Taos Rebellion.

The rebels murdered Governor Charles Bent, the sheriff of Taos, and his deputies, together with other prominent citizens. The army was called in to quell the rebellion, but this turned into an extremely bloody massacre of the rebels, many of whom were said to have been killed unnecessarily. In the spring of 1847 a semblance of peace was restored to the territory north of Santa Fe. Many of the trials and executions of the rebels were carried out in the federal court in Taos, the scene of the uprising.

In Washington however, Congress was worried about the still simmering resentment and the instability of the region in New Mexico and so in February 1848 they declared that the territory should have a military governor. The US Marshal was removed and the whole territory came under martial law and was 'policed' by the army.

There was bitter resentment from many of the prominent businessmen in the territory, who saw the introduction of a military governor as a major stumbling block to the formation of a new territorial government. They petitioned Congress demanding the removal of the military and the re-instatement of the Marshalcy. On 3 March 1851, the territory of New Mexico was created and the new territorial government installed – along with a new US Marshal.

The vast areas covered by the US Marshals are brought into perspective, when we consider that in 1851, US Marshal John G. Jones was appointed to enforce the law in Arizona and New Mexico. The land was inhabited by Indians, who recognised only their own laws; Mexicans, who were attuned to Mexican justice; and a sprinkling of Americans. The geography of the area ranged from mountain ranges to deserts, covered thousands of square miles and was virtually impossible to 'police'. Prudently, Marshal Jones confined his territory to the few large towns such as Santa Fe, Taos and Albuquerque, leaving the remaining territory, in effect, to fend for itself. There was one further town in the south of New Mexico, and that was Socorro, a haven for criminals, gunfighters and outlaws, and a town which no marshals relished the thought of entering. The only law there was the law of the gun, but surprisingly there are no recorded killings or attacks on marshals when they went to the town to serve warrants or to arrest suspects.

US Marshal's arrest warrant.

At each circuit session of a federal court, US Marshals opened the proceedings. The circuit of the court consisted of the judge, and other members of the bar, travelling from town to town to carry out their judicial duties, and they were almost always accompanied by either the marshal or his deputies.

US District Attorney William Watts Hart Davis recorded in his diary one such circuit in the spring of 1854, when, accompanied by Marshal Charles Blumner and other members of the judicial party, they covered over 1,000 miles in eight weeks on horseback, visiting seven major towns. At times the marshal would ride on ahead to prepare the towns for the arrival of the federal judge and his party, leaving his deputies to escort them.

In the towns and cities, the office of US Marshal was a prestigious one and required very little actual work for a very agreeable profit. Most of the work carried out within these cities was by the city or town marshal or his deputies who were paid a fixed wage. The deputy US Marshals, however, were usually paid on results and the type of work they were asked to do, so in order to earn a good living, the deputies were inclined to do most of the work. This of course enabled the US Marshal to continue with his own occupation and was also regarded as a stepping-stone to higher things.

In 1853 Congress drew up a fee list for US Marshals, which consisted of the following:

Wages per day for serving a court in session	$5.00
For drawing up and executing a deed	$5.00
Expenses incurred in chasing and arresting a criminal	$2.00 a day.
Escorting a prisoner to gaol	$0.10 per mile
Serving a warrant	$2.00
Serving a subpoena	$0.50
Bail bond	$0.50

Sheriffs on the other hand were paid a salary irrespective of what they did. There were perks, however, in the form of reward monies that were paid by the railroads, banks or stagecoach lines.

The remuneration to peace officers in these formative years was not good considering the hazardous work they were sometimes called upon to do. For example, the government paid the same fee to the marshal for the arrest of a harmless citizen, as for the arrest of a hardened and violent criminal. They couldn't, or wouldn't, differentiate between the two. The problem was that the people passing the legislation lived in relatively civilised cities, and had no concept of what it was like to live and work in some of the hostile environments of the West, where law and order was almost non-existent. There the 'law' was sometimes hundreds of miles away.

Territorial US Marshals had an annual salary of $200 and a $4,000 budget, and every cent spent had to be accounted for. Even this was not enough for the marshals to carry out their duties properly. The gaols to which the marshals were sometimes obliged to take their prisoners were sometimes nothing more than a shack with the door tied up with string to serve as a lock. In one incident in 1852 in Taos, New Mexico, the county officials declared that they had run out of money to feed the 14 prisoners being held in the local gaol. The local judge intervened and notified the governor that unless the marshal and local sheriff were supplied with more funds, the prisoners would die of starvation. Because there were no more funds available, the governor,

A typical town gaol.

very reluctantly, was forced to pardon the prisoners, but with the proviso that they left the territory within 25 days.

This was a problem that was not going to go away, and proposals were put forward for the building of a state prison. It was to be funded by the government, thus taking the responsibility of the welfare of prisoners away from the restricted budgets of the marshals and sheriffs. But it was to take a further 30 years before the prison was eventually built in 1885.

The vast majority of sheriffs and US Marshals worked together, but of course there were some cases of resentment by sheriffs when they thought some of the marshals coming into their district were undermining their authority. In general, however, the law enforcement officers worked well together.

Pursuing criminals was an onerous task in many ways. The marshal usually had to put together an armed posse to track him, or on some rare occasions her, down. This was made difficult because he rarely knew anybody and most people did not want to get involved. The marshal did however have the power to command a citizen or citizens to join him in the posse. Although in films when the sheriff needed a posse the local townspeople always seemed to immediately spring to his aid and gallop off in hot pursuit, this was not always the case. In fact it usually took some time to get a posse or comitatus, as it was officially known, together, and they had to be paid.

In 1853 Marshal Charles Rumley, who covered the district in which the community of Mesilla was situated, found himself in an impossible situation. In the village of Don Ana, inhabited by Apache Indians, a number of Mexicans attacked the Indians there, killing the chief. The village lay within a disputed area of Mexico, so when Marshal Rumley asked the Mexicans to arrest the killers, they refused. Together with the local sheriff, a posse was organised. They then asked for assistance from soldiers at the local fort, Fort Fillmore. The post commander refused, stating that it was a civilian affair and had nothing to do with the army, and also that any incursion by the army into the disputed territory could be seen by the Mexicans as an act of aggression by the United States. Faced with an impossible situation, the marshal gave up, disbanded the posse and the hunt for the killers was abandoned. The murderers were never brought to justice.

In Kansas, during President Franklin Pierce's term of office, there was widespread resistance to the marshals when serious violence sprang up between two pro- and anti-slavery factions. The marshals found it almost impossible to get a posse together to catch the law-breakers, as they either supported one side or the other. This necessitated the President assigning a troop of cavalry to the territory to ensure that there was a posse ready if needed. The power to do this came from an incident in 1807, when President Thomas Jefferson ordered the army to assist marshals when Congress encountered opposition to its Embargo Act.

The problems of New Mexico and its Hispanic population were still cause for some concern, but US Marshal Charles P. Clever eased the situation somewhat by appointing Sheriff Jesus Maria Sena y Baca, a Hispanic, as his deputy. Baca spoke both Mexican and English and could relate comfortably to the Hispanic communities in the territory.

At the beginning of the American Civil War (1861–1865) or 'The War Between the States', as it is sometimes referred to, almost all the US Marshals throughout the South resigned because of their support for the Confederacy. This highlighted the problem of selecting candidates from the states in which they were to serve.

The Civil War forced marshals and sheriffs in the south to decide where their loyalties lay: to the government of the day, or to their communities. Those who chose the federal government rode a very dangerous line when trying to carry out their duties and enforce the law. It also extended their areas of responsibility and invariably put them into conflict with both sides. This manifested itself when Congress passed two acts, the 'First and Second Confiscation Acts', which called for the seizure of property deemed to be of use, or used, by the Confederacy. This was later amended so that although officers of the Confederacy had all their property confiscated, sympathisers could redeem their property if they showed allegiance to the Union within 60 days.

As became obvious later, this law was abused when mines, cattle and other lucrative possessions were confiscated under the umbrella of this act. One marshal, Abraham Cutler, was said to have 'confiscated' $500,000 worth of property and goods in Texas during 1864. He then was alleged to have forged letters from 'informants', who were entitled to some of the proceeds and bought the property from them in his wife's name. The result was that a number of court hearings took place when the owners of the property and goods claimed that they had been defrauded. Cutler was found guilty on a number of the charges and ordered to return the deeds of property confiscated, but not guilty of some of the other lesser charges.

Despite his personal feelings for the South, Marshal Cutler continued to carry out his duties with dedication. When approached by a senior Union officer, who stated that southern spies were infiltrating some of his already nervous volunteer territorial units causing morale problems, he took steps to find them – and did.

The law in these formative years was fraught with problems, both for the accused and the lawman. In 1862, a gambler by the name of William Mayfield was accused of giving shelter to a gunman by the name of Henry Plummer. The sheriff of Ormsby County and a former Deputy US Marshal was John Blackburn, a man with a reputation for being a bully and a drunk. Unable to find any evidence to connect Mayfield with Plummer, Blackburn picked a fight with Mayfield in a saloon and threatened him with a gun. Realising that Mayfield didn't carry a gun, Blackburn started to pistol-whip him. In fear of his life, Mayfield pulled out a Bowie knife and stabbed Blackburn to death. Even though there were witnesses to say that it was an act committed in self-defence, Mayfield was arrested. After a short trial, at which no witnesses were called or questioned, and in which the prosecution revealed that Mayfield was a southern sympathiser, he was convicted and sentenced to hang. There was not one southerner on the jury, which pre-empted the guilty verdict somewhat. While awaiting the result of his appeal in the state prison, he managed to escape with the help of some southern sympathisers, and made his way over the Sierra Mountains to Carson City. The new sheriff of Ormsby County followed him to Carson City, but the local residents had been made aware of the injustice and refused to reveal his whereabouts. The sheriff and his posse had to give up their pursuit and return to Ormsby County.

In an effort to maintain law and order, which had been threatened by the mass resignations of the marshals in the South, the Confederate States of America set up federal district courts. Each of these court districts appointed a Confederate States Marshal, who in turn appointed his own deputies. Little is known about the work of these men, possibly because after the war there were few survivors and most of the records had been destroyed, but without their dedication there is no doubt that martial law would have had to be introduced.

The selection of a US Marshal at this time depended largely on which political party he supported, his local standing in the community in which he lived, and his knowledge of the people in the district in which he was to serve. Of course it helped considerably if the candidate supported the President's political party, thus ensuring that any policies put forward would be rigidly enforced. Sheriffs, on the other hand, were not aligned to any political party and did not have to have local knowledge, but it was an asset to know the people you were dealing with.

During the civil war life in America continued as normally as it could and the local sheriffs still struggled to maintain law and order, especially in the small mining towns. In one such mining community, Dayton, Nevada, a small, but very respectable town, the citizens meted out their own brand of justice when one of their number was brutally murdered. A man by the name of John Doyle ran a saloon and dance hall frequented by miners. One evening a customer called Linn got drunk and started an argument, which quickly flared into a fight when Doyle tried to remove him. Linn pulled out a knife and stabbed Doyle in the heart. He was quickly seized by other customers and marched to the local gaol. The local citizens, enraged by the incident, decided that a trial was unnecessary and during the night secretly built a set of gallows. During the night a party of vigilantes entered the gaol, and took Linn out. To stop him screaming they filled his mouth with dirt and then they hanged him. When he was dead, they took him down and returned his body to his cell.

The next morning when the sheriff opened the cell he was astonished to find Linn's body sprawled across his bed. The incident had the effect of clearing out almost all the transients and undesirables from the town, but word filtered through to Governor Nye, who immediately dispatched a troop of soldiers to the town to 'restore and maintain law and order'. When the soldiers arrived they found one of the most peaceful towns in the West. The Governor arrived some days later to read the riot act out to the citizens, but found he was reading it to a deserted main street. He left the same day.

Main Street of Dayton, Nevada in 1880.

This incident demonstrated that the citizens of these towns were not prepared to put up with violence and murder, and if the law couldn't put a stop to it, then they would. Slowly but surely, the lawlessness that had blighted the country for so many years was being brought under control.

At the end of the Civil War, the marshals and sheriffs in the South were at the forefront of helping the reconstruction of the southern states, which lay in tatters. They also had to deal with the problem of the illicit distilling of hard liquor and its distribution, which was becoming an extremely lucrative business. In the north and east of the country, 'Lynch Law' was still being carried out and slaves, who had tried to escape under the cover of the war and had been recaptured, were often lynched and castrated as a warning to others, and left to hang in the hot sun for days on end. Lynching was not restricted to runaway slaves, but included anyone caught stealing or suspected of stealing.

The areas now patrolled by US Marshals covered hundreds of square miles and they were no longer known to many of the inhabitants, most of whom were illiterate, so it was no good showing them a piece of paper stating their authority. In order to identify themselves as lawmen, the vast majority of the marshals made their own badges out of whatever materials came to hand, such as copper, brass, tin and so on, and they were roughly made. As one convicted criminal put it after being captured: 'The marshals were rougher than the badges they wore'.

Most of the badges were in the shape of a star, the same as the sheriffs', but there were a small number made in the shape of a shield. It wasn't until 1941 that an official standardised US Marshals badge was introduced and issued to all members of the US Marshals Service (USMS). There were three models, United States Marshal, Chief Deputy United States Marshal and Deputy United States Marshal. All were numbered on the reverse side. Sheriffs' badges also varied in design and construction, depending on what the town elders decided upon. The vast majority were in the shape of a star in the smaller towns, but city marshal's badges were often in the shape of a shield.

In 1870 the Department of Justice was created and all control of law enforcement was placed in its hands. This released the marshals from the confines of the political structure, and gave them greater authority and wider latitude in the way they dispensed the law.

The Civil War, however, had decimated the male population and created lawlessness among the many transients that roamed the country.

Above left: Lincoln County Sheriff's badge.

Above right: Deputy US Marshal's shield.

Many of these were soldiers from the South who had lost everything: their families, friends, homes, and businesses. The war was a major event that was to bring a social change that would ultimately shape America's future, and facilitate the freedom and ongoing struggle for equality for all Americans.

However the myths, legends and real history of the Wild West also continue to fascinate the imagination and provide controversy and inspiration. The 'Good and the Bad' elements battling for supremacy have always been an enduring and rewarding study for civilisation throughout history.

Chapter 1

Robert Forsyth

United States Marshal Robert Forsyth was the first US Marshal in the state of Georgia and had served there for four years. A veteran of the Revolutionary War, he had fought the British throughout the long conflict and was more than capable of taking care of himself. On 11 January 1794, the 40-year-old Robert Forsyth was sent to a house in Augusta, Georgia, to serve some civil court papers on two brothers, Beverley and William Allen.

This was a routine assignment and one that was usually carried out alone, but, unusually, Forsyth took two of his deputies with him and on arriving, entered the house. The Allen brothers were talking with friends and on seeing the marshal and his deputies, for some unknown reason, they fled up the stairs and locked themselves in a room. The federal officers gave chase and, as they approached the room, Beverley Allen fired through the door and hit Robert Forsyth in the head, killing him instantly. The two brothers were arrested after a brief fight and put in the local gaol, but within days they had escaped and were never caught – some think this was due to aid by the local sheriff.

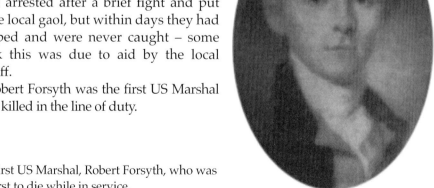

Robert Forsyth was the first US Marshal to be killed in the line of duty.

The first US Marshal, Robert Forsyth, who was the first to die while in service.

Chapter 2

Colonel Charles Lynch

'Lynch Law' is said to have been created by Colonel Charles Lynch, a Quaker who served in the American Revolution (1776–1783) under General Nathaniel Greene. Colonel Lynch and a number of other planters in Virginia were becoming increasingly concerned by the lack of law and order and subsequent justice, and so they formed their own justice system. Anyone caught stealing horses or cattle, or indeed committing any crime, was hauled before Colonel Lynch and three of his neighbours and tried in a court in Lynch's house. If convicted, which they invariably were, punishment was carried out almost immediately. If the punishment meted out by the court was a flogging, the prisoner

was taken into the backyard, hung from a branch of a tree by his thumbs, given 39 lashes and ordered to leave the county. If a death sentence was passed he was simply taken out and hanged.

Despite these actions being totally illegal, crime in the area reduced dramatically and the government turned a blind eye to the proceedings, which became known as 'Lynch's Law'. The problem was that once it started, and was given an unofficial 'blessing' by the government of the day, it became almost impossible to stop. As people from Virginia migrated to other parts of the United States, they tended to

Colonel Charles Lynch.

take the use of 'Lynch's Law' with them. This is how the expression 'Lynch Law' is said to have been derived.

All the US Marshals, deputy marshals, sheriffs and deputy sheriffs who policed the Indian Territories (Eastern Oklahoma) in the late 1800s took their prisoners for trial and sentence to Fort Smith. There they faced one of the most famous judges in America – Judge Isaac Parker.

Chapter 3

Judge Isaac Parker

Isaac Parker was the youngest son of Joseph Parker and his wife Jane Shannon, and the great-nephew of Ohio Governor Wilson Shannon. He was raised on the family farm near Barnesville, Ohio. He attended Breeze Hill Primary School, followed by the Barnesville Classical Institute, a private school. In order to pay for his secondary education Isaac Parker taught in a county primary school. At the age of 17, he began an apprenticeship in law, and passed the Ohio bar exam in 1859.

On completion of his law degree, Isaac Parker went to work for his maternal uncle's law firm in St Joseph, Missouri. He married Mary O'Toole on 12 December 1861 and the couple had two sons, Charles and James. A year after starting work for his uncle he opened his own law firm, working mainly in the municipal and country courts. He also ran successfully as the Democrat nomination for the position of St Joseph City Attorney, which was a part-time appointment, and he served three one-year terms in the post from 1861 to 1863. Just four days after taking up the appointment the American Civil War broke out. Isaac Parker immediately enlisted in the 61st Missouri Emergency Regiment, which was a pro-union home guard, and by the end of the war he had reached the rank of corporal.

Portrait shot of Judge Isaac Parker.

Returning to his law practice full time, he decided to split his time between law and politics after leaving the Democratic Party over their views on slavery and joining the Republican Party. He became the county prosecutor for the Ninth Missouri Judicial District and then in 1868 won a six-year term as a judge on the Twelfth Missouri Circuit. However, politics was still his main interest and at the end of 1870 he resigned his position as a judge. Backed by the Republican Party he was voted into the United States House of Representatives, where he served for five years. At the end of his term of office he became the party's nominee for the Missouri Senate seat, but the political tide had shifted away from the Republicans so he made representation to the President for the appointment as a judge for the Western District of Arkansas.

On 26 May 1874, President Ulysses S. Grant appointed him to serve on the United States District Court for the Western District of Arkansas to replace Judge William Story, who had resigned under the threat of impeachment because of allegations of corruption. The United States Senate confirmed the appointment in November 1874.

Judge Isaac Parker arrived in Fort Smith on 4 May 1875, initially without his family, who joined him some weeks later. It took just one week for him to settle down and have his first session as the district judge. During the month of May Judge Parker tried 18 men, all of whom had been charged with murder: 15 were convicted by a jury, and of those 15, eight were given the death penalty and six of them were hanged at the same time. One of the eight was shot trying to escape, while the other had his sentence commuted to life in prison. The remaining seven were given long prison sentences. In an interview, Judge Parker was asked how he felt about sending someone to the gallows: he replied that he didn't, the law did that because of the mandatory death sentence set down for certain cases. He himself was

Judge Isaac Parker sitting in his famous chair.

in favour of the abolition of capital punishment, but he was obliged by law to pass sentence as laid down.

Judge Isaac Parker spent 21 years on the bench as a federal judge (1875–1896) in Arkansas, during which time he tried almost 13,500 cases, almost all of which had been committed in the Indian Territories. Out of the 9,500 criminals found guilty or who had pleaded guilty, 160 had committed crimes that carried the death sentence, and of these only 79 were actually hanged. It was this large number of hangings that gave Isaac Parker the unfair title of the 'Hanging Judge', but all were said to have been justified, as he was known to be a very fair man who kept rigidly to the letter of the law. He was the only judge for hundreds of miles, so any sentence he passed would have no comparison to anything else in a wide area.

On arriving at Fort Smith to take up his appointment, Isaac Parker set about building a legal team to support him, starting with the chief prosecutor William H. Clayton who was to remain as the United States Attorney for the Western District of Arkansas for the next 14 years. Clayton had fought in the Civil War with the 124th Pennsylvania Infantry with

The courtroom in Fort Smith.

distinction, and together with his assistant James Brizzolara they made a formidable team. Isaac Parker took up residence just 300 metres from the courthouse in a large stone building formerly used to store gunpowder. The main window of the house had an uninterrupted view of the large, sturdily built gallows from which Judge Parker could see justice being done. The gallows structure allowed a maximum of 12 persons, standing side by side, to be hanged together. Later a roof was built over the top so that the gallows could be used even in inclement weather.

When Judge Isaac Parker stepped onto the bench he had to try and maintain law

William H. Clayton, chief prosecutor in Isaac Parker's court at Fort Smith.

The Fort Smith commissary building used by Judge Isaac Parker as his living quarters.

The faithfully reconstructed gallows at Fort Smith.

and order over 74,000 square miles with just 200 Deputy US Marshals. His instructions to his deputies were to 'bring them in alive or dead', the latter not being the best option financially, as is explained later. The deputies were chasing criminals and outlaws who knew every trail and hideout and their only weapons were their bravery, dedication and their skill with a gun. Furthermore, these deputies sometimes had to transport prisoners back to Fort Smith over several hundred miles. They also suffered setbacks when ordinary citizens would refuse to allow a deputy and his prisoners shelter, for fear of reprisals from friends of the arrested man.

Hangings in earlier years had taken on an almost carnival atmosphere and this was seen when the first of Judge Parker's hangings took place. Six men, three white, two Indians and a black man, were sentenced to be hanged at Fort Smith. Six men being hanged at the same time was so unusual that it was covered by almost all the newspapers, and over 5,000 people travelled hundreds of miles to witness the executions. After this debacle, a concerned Judge Parker ordered that the only people who would be allowed to witness an execution would be issued with passes, and these were only to be issued to necessary witnesses of the hangings.

Murderers Gilbert and Rosengrants being hanged in front of an enormous crowd of onlookers in Leadville, Colorado. It was this kind of 'carnival' atmosphere that prompted Judge Isaac Parker to order that all executions at Fort Smith would only be attended by those required to be there to witness it.

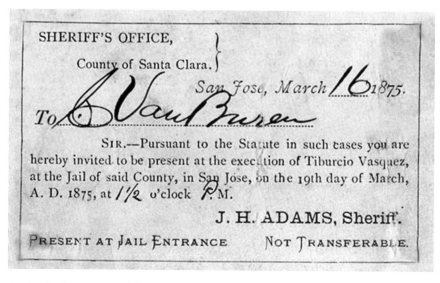

SHERIFF'S OFFICE,
County of Santa Clara.
San Jose, March 16 1875.

To

Sir.—Pursuant to the Statute in such cases you are hereby invited to be present at the execution of Tiburcio Vasquez, at the Jail of said County, in San Jose, on the 19th day of March, A. D. 1875, at 1½ o'clock P. M.

J. H. ADAMS, Sheriff.

PRESENT AT JAIL ENTRANCE   NOT TRANSFERABLE.

An invitation to attend the execution of Tiburcio Vasquez.

US Marshals carried out the first hangings at Fort Smith, but as more and more criminals were sent to the gallows, the need for a hangman became obvious. The marshals attached to Fort Smith complained that

it was taking up too much of their time and that they would be better off chasing other criminals. The man who volunteered for the position was George Maledon, a prison guard at Fort Smith. A former immigrant from Bavaria, he became an expert at his chosen profession, carrying out the executions in a humane way. But because of the nature of his profession, he found himself shunned by the townspeople in the town in which he lived. George Maledon prided himself on being an expert hangman, making sure that

George Maledon, Fort Smith prison guard, who became the official hangman.

10

James-Fleming-Parker, the last man to be hanged at the courthouse plaza in Prescott, Arizona.

the prisoner's neck was broken when he was dropped and not slowly strangled as happened in most lynchings.

In smaller towns, hundreds of miles from large towns and cities, it was the duty of the local sheriff or town marshal to carry out executions. Local people, who had been sworn in as deputies just in case there was an attempt by some of the condemned man's friends or relatives to release him, usually assisted them. One such execution took place on 16 March 1900 in Fergus County, Montana. On 25 March 1899 a man by the name of Billy Calder was convicted of the murder of Farquar McRae and John Allen and sentenced to death. Deputy Sheriff Lincoln P. Slater hanged Billy Calder in the Lewiston Gaol yard under the watchful eye of a Dr Wilson and a number of deputies. Fourteen minutes elapsed before Billy Calder was pronounced dead. This was the first and last 'legal' hanging to take place in Fergus County, Montana. The scaffold was unusual because a weight, via a series of pulleys, was dropped to jerk the condemned man upwards so that his feet were only inches from the floor, as can be seen in the photographs.

11

Above left: Billy Calder, about to be hanged for murder in courtyard of Ferguson County Gaol, Montana. This was an unusual method of execution in which the convicted murderer was jerked upwards by the rope going through a series of pulleys when the weight in the left hand side of the photograph was dropped.

Above right: Billy Calder's body hanging just inches from the floor after his execution.

In 1887 a document was issued listing 'Laws Governing US Marshals', which showed that his role consisted of:

- *Serving Writs of Possession, Bench Warrants, and Warrants of Attachment*
- *Serving Subpoenas, Summonses and Complaints*
- *Rescuing seized property*
- *Making arrests for:*
    - Introducing liquor onto an Indian Reservation
    - Obstructing free passage through Public Lands
    - Cutting Wood on Government Land
    - Robbing a Post Office
    - Murder
    - Defrauding the Revenue by smuggling cigars

For the first 100 years of the service, the marshal employed as few, or as many, deputies as he felt he needed. The deputies were paid using a fee system depending on what they were required to do: serving warrants, writs or summonses or chasing after criminals and arresting them. This gave rise to the saying *'The greater the risk, the greater the pay'*. In 1896, Congress decided that they should all have salaries and did away with the fee system. The Attorney General's office also restricted the number of deputies a marshal could employ, unless circumstances dictated otherwise, and then only with their approval.

The period between the end of the Civil War and the beginning of the 1900s was the most turbulent and violent for the marshals, and the casualty rate they suffered was greater than any time before or after this period. It was then that the recognition of the marshals' contribution to law and order really came to the fore, with stories of their exploits, and in some cases, their notoriety.

There were also a number of lesser-known law enforcement officers who carried out their work without fame, or notoriety, yet still managed to be feared among the law-breaking fraternity. One of these was Burton Mossman, who operated in New Mexico.

Chapter 4

Burton Mossman

Burton Mossman had started his working life, like many others at the time, as a cowboy. It was during a period when the ranch he was working on suffered a number of rustling episodes that Mossman found that he had a natural aptitude for finding the thieves. He came to the attention of the sheriff of a small town called Holbrook when he brought in three rustlers whom he had tracked down and captured after they had taken cattle from the ranch on which he had been working. Rustling in the area at the time was a source of some concern to the ranchers, and, fearing that they might start to take the law into their own hands, Sheriff Wattron appointed Mossman as his deputy and assigned him specifically to tracking the rustlers down.

It was known that a band of Mexicans and renegade Mormons was operating in the area, and it was these that Mossman went after. Within months the number of rustling raids had been reduced and most of the rustlers were languishing in gaol. One of the most notorious rustlers at the time was a man by the name of Bill Young. Mossman had been after him for months, but could not get enough evidence to arrest him. After a number of rustlers had been arrested and convicted, Young suddenly

Portrait shot of Captain Burton C. Mossman of the Arizona Rangers.

announced that he had had enough of 'that damned Mossman' and headed for Colorado. Burton Mossman was invited to join the Arizona Rangers, a law enforcement agency created by Governor Murphy, and was given the rank of captain. Their first assignment was to investigate a post office robbery carried out by a notorious criminal by the name of Bill Smith, with his gang.

Within days Mossman and four other Rangers had cornered the gang: two were arrested while the remaining three escaped. The gang later held up the Union Pacific train at Utah and, during a gunfight with three Rangers, two of the Rangers were shot dead.

Mossman, with the help of two Indian trackers, went after the gang, but they had split up and Bill Smith had headed for Mexico. One Ranger, Sergeant Dayton Graham, who was patrolling the border, was informed of a suspicious-looking man hanging around in Douglas, a town close to the border on the American side. Graham and the town marshal approached the man, but before they could speak to him he drew his gun and shot the marshal through the neck, killing him, and then shot the Ranger through his left arm and lung.

Graham survived the shooting and for two months lay recovering in bed, vowing to find and kill the man who shot had him and the town marshal. Mossman, who visited Graham, obtained a description of the man they were after. It was Bill Smith, the man Mossman had been trailing for months. Graham, after recovering from his wounds, went

Above left: Arizona Rangers captain's badge.

Above right: Captain Burton C. Mossman at his desk.

looking for Smith from town to town. One night he entered a small-town saloon, and there at a card table was Smith, the man who had gunned him and the town marshal down so ruthlessly. Smith looked up, immediately realised that he had been spotted and went for his gun, but Graham already had his gun out of its holster and he put a bullet through Bill Smith's head. Walking up to the lifeless body on the floor, Graham fired two more bullets into the man's body – just to make sure.

Another of the exploits of Mossman and his Rangers was when six 'respectable citizens' from a town called Globe were involved in cattle rustling, and were arrested by the Rangers. The other citizens of the town were so incensed by the manner in which their fellow citizens had been arrested that they put up 2,000 dollars bail for each of the men. The men were released and almost immediately headed for Mexico. When their trial came up, they were nowhere to be found and the upright citizens of Globe had to forfeit the bail money. They immediately petitioned the Governor for the return of the money, but the Governor placed the decision in the hands of Captain Mossman. He refused to return it, saying that the citizens should have thought twice before putting up bail for 'respected citizens' and that the bail money was now forfeit under the law.

Mossman and his Arizona Rangers went on to keep law and order throughout the state and enjoyed a reputation that put fear into whoever they were looking for. Burton Mossman died on 5 September 1956 in New Mexico at the age of 89.

Arizona Rangers.

Chapter 5

James Butler Hickok

There were many famous names associated with the US Marshals, such as James Butler Hickok, also known as 'Wild Bill Hickok', who, in 1865, was a deputy marshal at Fort Riley, Kansas. His fearsome reputation was coupled with his formidable appearance: he was over 6ft tall, and of large build, which stopped most drunks or troublemakers from upsetting him. He also had shoulder-length blond hair and a moustache

Above left: Head and shoulders portrait shot of James Butler Hickok.

Above right: Wild Bill Hickok wearing his pair of reversed ivory-handled Colts and a large hunting knife tucked in his belt.

and sometimes dressed as a river gambler, with a long black coat and fancy waistcoat that contrasted well with his hair and moustache. He also carried two ivory-handled pistols, a large Bowie knife and a sawn-off shotgun, which ensured respect from the rowdiest of people.

Hickok was always depicted in books at the time, and later on screen, as the epitome of a fearless lawman, but this was far from the truth. He had a tarnished reputation, which covered rustling, gambling, gun-fighting and murder. He was tried on several occasions for murder, but never convicted.

He became an army scout in August 1861 and was involved in a number of spying missions for the Union Army. He was once again accused of murder in 1865, when, in a shoot-out in the main street of Springfield, Missouri, he gunned down a gambler by the name of Davis K. Tutt. After a short trial he was acquitted when it was decided that he had acted in self-defence.

Hickok was appointed a Deputy US Marshal at Fort Riley from 1867 to 1869, and then was city marshal of Fort Hays for a brief period in 1869. He enforced a new ordinance against the carrying of weapons, by patrolling the streets, wearing buckskins and carrying his two pistols, his large Bowie knife, and his sawn-off shotgun. He presented an imposing and threatening figure as he patrolled the streets.

There were a number of unsavoury incidents in which he was involved during this time, concerning shoot-outs in gambling halls, but during the last incident, four soldiers from the fort were killed. General Sheridan ordered his immediate arrest, but Hickok fled.

In 1871 he turned up in Abilene, Kansas and took up the post of city marshal. His reputation had gone before him and it is on record that on the very day he took office he killed two men. He also came up against John Wesley Hardin during an argument in a card game, but such were their reputations, that neither wanted to settle it with guns. One gunman, Phil Cole, who confronted Hickok in the street, suffered the consequences when he refused to hand over his gun and was shot dead. But during one frantic gun battle in the street, Hickok accidentally

An early shot of James Butler Hickok – Wild Bill Hickok.

shot Deputy Marshal Mike Williams. It is not known whether or not the wound was fatal.

Shortly afterwards Hickok left Abilene and joined Buffalo Bill's 'Scout of the Plains' show which was touring the West at the time, but he left after a few months and returned to his old ways.

In 1873 Hickok returned to Fort Hayes as marshal for a short time, before heading up to Deadwood during the Dakota gold rush period.

On 1 August 1876 Hickok was playing cards in Nuttal & Mann's Saloon in Deadwood when one of the players dropped out. Jack McCall, who had been drinking for most of the day and was drunk, took his place. McCall was very soon broke and Hickok, feeling sorry for him, offered him some money to get some food. McCall accepted the money but felt he had been cheated and insulted by the offer. The following evening Hickok was once again at the card table with his back to the door, which was not his normal way of sitting when playing cards, as he almost always sat with his back against the wall. The saloon doors swung open and an extremely drunk Jack McCall staggered in, pointed a single-action revolver at the back of Hickok's head and pulled the trigger, shouting, 'Damn you. Take that'. Hickok died instantly. McCall then ran into the street and tried to steal a horse, but was so drunk he fell off. A search for McCall started and he was found hiding in the back of a shop. During his trial McCall claimed that he shot Hickok in revenge for the killing of his brother in Abilene, Kansas. McCall was later hanged for the murder of Wild Bill Hickok.

Writers, trying to glamorise the West for their readers, exaggerated almost all of Wild Bill Hickok's exploits during his time as a lawman. The larger than life characters they created out of real people created a lot of myths, although later historians would discover the truth.

Postcard of James Butler Hickok (Wild Bill).

Phil Coe.

Chapter 6

Henry Andrew 'Heck' Thomas

One of the most respected lawmen of the time was Henry Andrew 'Heck' Thomas. His friends gave him the nickname of 'Heck', because it was the only 'cussword' he was ever heard to utter, even under the most trying circumstances.

Born on 6 January 1850 in Oxford, Georgia, Heck Thomas joined the Confederate Army at the age of 12 as a courier to General 'Stonewall' Jackson. The end of the war saw the South desolated and jobs hard to find, especially for southerners. In 1868 Heck Thomas became a city policeman in Atlanta, Georgia and it was here, during a particularly violent riot, that he first used his gun and was injured in the process.

He then took a job as an express messenger with the Texas Express Company, and it was while working for them that he came in contact with the notorious Sam Bass gang. They specialised in carrying out train robberies and it was during one of these that Heck Thomas came up with the idea of switching any money that was being carried with fake money in the event of a hold-up. His idea came to fruition on the evening of 18 March 1878, when the Bass gang held up a train on which he was supervising a large amount

US Deputy Marshal 'Heck' Thomas.

of cash. Thomas managed to secrete the real cash and substitute it for fake money. The gang took a bag of silver dollars and the fake money, and got away with just $100. Thomas received a $200 reward from the company for saving the cash.

Leaving the express company in 1885, Heck Thomas joined the Fort Worth Detective Agency. One of his first jobs was to join up with Deputy US Marshal Jim Taylor in an effort to track down the Lee brothers, who were wanted for murder.

Information regarding the whereabouts of the brothers led Thomas and Taylor to a remote farmhouse near Dexter, Texas. Finding the place deserted, the two lawmen decided to lie in wait for a few days, convinced that the information given to them was correct. Five days later the two brothers, Pink and Jim Lee, rode up and, after a brief exchange of gunfire, both outlaws were killed. The reward for the two brothers was a sizeable one, which convinced Heck Thomas that bounty hunting seemed like a very lucrative occupation.

Above left: Bill Thomas.

Above right: Deputy US Marshal 'Heck' Thomas with members of his posse.

After his work on the Lee case, Heck Thomas was offered the post of Deputy US Marshal, which he readily accepted, and it was a job he was to carry out for the next 26 years.

His first job was to buy himself a pair of Colt 45 Peacemaker revolvers and a Winchester Model 1886 45–90. These weapons were to be with him for the remainder of his lawman days. In the following years Heck Thomas was to be involved in some of the most famous arrests and gun battles of the West, including the capture of the infamous Dalton gang. Towards the end of the century the outlaw bands had all but disappeared and the only one left, of any notoriety, was Bill Doolin.

Heck Thomas picked up Doolin's trail and followed him to Oklahoma, where he caught up with him at a house near Lawton. Calling on him to surrender, he was met with a refusal and Doolin opened fire on Thomas. Heck Thomas blasted him with his 12-gauge shotgun and the last of the Doolin gang was dead.

Heck Thomas worked as a deputy marshal in Oklahoma Territory after leaving Fort Smith, where he met up with Bill Tilghman and

 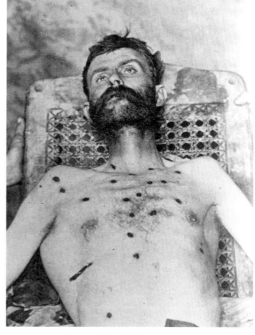

Above left: William 'Bill' Doolin.

Above right: Bill Doolin's shotgun-peppered body.

Chris Madsen. In the following three years they arrested more than 300 wanted men. It is said that Heck Thomas picked the most dangerous desperadoes to go after because of the large rewards on their heads.

In 1902 Heck Thomas moved to Lawton, Oklahoma Territory, where he was appointed Chief of Police, and for the next seven years he maintained law and order there. He was wounded half a dozen times in gunfights during his career as a lawman. In 1909 he suffered a heart attack and retired. He died on 15 August 1912 of Bright's disease.

Chapter 7

Bill Tilghman

Unlike many lawmen, including Wyatt Earp, Bill Tilghman had an unblemished record throughout his career as a lawman. Born on 4 July 1854, he worked the family farm while his father and brothers were away fighting in the Civil War, and it was during this time that he met Wild Bill Hickok. Hickok had observed the young Bill Tilghman practising his shooting and had taught him the art of drawing his gun fast and accurately, a skill that was to stand him in good stead in the future. Tilghman started his working life as a buffalo hunter, killing over 7,000 of the animals over two years, almost doubling `Buffalo' Bill Cody's record. Among the group of buffalo hunters with whom he worked were the Masterson brothers, Bat, Jim and Ed. Bat Masterson was later to find fame as a lawman and gunfighter.

Becoming disillusioned with the months of living in the wilderness, Bill Tilghman headed for Dodge City, one of the roughest towns in the West at the time. On arrival the sheriff, an old friend by the name of Charlie Bassett, greeted him. This was the last person he had expected to see and Bassett, who knew of Tilghman's reputation, immediately offered him the deputy sheriff's job. Within hours news had spread of the new deputy in town who

A young Deputy US Marshal Bill Tilghman.

24

never carried a gun. The first test of his ability came when one of the local gunmen confronted him. The local ordinance stated that it was an offence to carry a gun in the town and the local 'tough guy' was wearing his. Tilghman told him that he was to hand his guns over until he left town as it was against the law. The reply came quickly, 'You want them, come and get them'. Before the tough guy could move Bill Tilghman hit him with one punch that sent him crashing to the floor. He was then carted off to gaol and that was the end of his attempt to show the deputy who was boss in the town!

Right: Bill Tilghman when he was a buffalo hunter in the Indian Territories.

Below: Dodge City in 1875.

It was around this time that Bat Masterson arrived in town and he too was quickly taken on as a deputy sheriff. Between the three of them they slowly quelled the violence and disorder in Dodge City, and despite the frequent visits of such gunmen as Ben Thompson, Doc Holliday and John Wesley Hardin, it remained a relatively peaceful town.

In 1878, Bat Masterson became sheriff of Ford County, Kansas, and he asked Bill Tilghman to remain his deputy. For the next six years the pair of them kept strict law and order in the town, before Tilghman was offered the post of town marshal of Dodge City, which he accepted and carried out with the same efficiency.

After five years in the post, Tilghman and his family moved to Guthrie, Oklahoma Territory, where he was to take up the post of marshal. Because of the land rush in the territory, the town was full of every type of person one could imagine: land speculators; families trying to start a new life; gamblers; prostitutes and gunmen. The town

Deputy US Marshal Bill Tilghman.

Above: Deputy US Marshal Bill Tilghman on his horse, preparing to head out into the Indian Territory.

Right: Deputy US Marshal Bill Tilghman with his weapons.

was packed to capacity with squatters clogging up the main street. Tilghman and his deputy Jim Masterson, together with a number of other local citizens, cleared the main street by dragging chained logs down the street, clearing everything and everybody away. The fact that Bill Tilghman was riding slowly in front carrying a 12-gauge shotgun may have also had something to do with the rapid exodus.

The town soon realised that they had a lawman who would stand no nonsense, and slowly but surely he cleaned out all the undesirables and helped to bring a semblance of normality to the town. His fame as a lawman spread throughout the territory and in 1883 he was asked by US Marshal Bill Grimes to be a Deputy US Marshal. This gave Bill Tilghman a regular salary of around $400 a year plus expenses.

The Doolin gang was possibly the biggest thorn in the side of the law in Oklahoma, and they always seemed to be one step ahead of any attempt to capture them. That was until one of the gang, by the name of 'Arkansas Tom' Daugherty, was captured during an abortive raid in the town of Ingalls. In an effort to cooperate with the law and

gain a possible reduction in sentence when he came to trial, Daugherty told them of two young girls called Cattle Annie and Little Breeches, who besides being petty thieves also gave information to the Doolin gang about the marshal and sheriff's movements.

Tilghman found out where the girls were and together with Steve Burke, another deputy marshal, went after them. They followed a trail to a farmhouse where, as they approached,

Left: Tom Daugherty.

Below: Murray's Saloon in Ingalls.

one of the girls, Little Breeches, jumped on a horse and headed out. Tilghman gave chase and, despite being fired upon by the girl, managed to capture her. Steve Burke managed to subdue the other girl after a violent struggle. Both girls were sent to the federal reformatory at Framingham for a number of years.

Things remained reasonably quiet for the next few years, but then the Doolin-Dalton gang appeared and started to terrorise a number of the states. Three Deputy US Marshals, Bill Tilghman, Heck Thomas and Chris Madsen, were assigned to track them down and bring the gang to justice – dead or alive. Then, during a bank raid in Southwest City, Missouri, when a local politician was gunned down, the word 'alive' was removed from the judge's warrant. For the next three years, the three men tracked the gang from state to state, until on 15 January 1895, word reached Bill Tilghman that Bill Doolin was in Eureka Springs, Arkansas.

Having travelled for many hours, Tilghman decided to enjoy one of the hot baths the town was famous for providing, before looking for Doolin. As he entered the lobby of the bathhouse, there stretched out on a couch reading a newspaper was Bill Doolin. Whipping out his revolver, Tilghman thrust the barrel of the gun in Doolin's face and said

'Bill Doolin, you're under arrest. I am Deputy US Marshal Tilghman and I am going to take you back to Guthrie to stand trial'.

Doolin made to go for his revolver, which was in a shoulder holster, but thought better of it when Tilghman said,

'Don't do it Doolin, I don't want to shoot you, but I will if I have to'.

Doolin was handcuffed with the help of the local sheriff, who had been called by the receptionist, and taken to the local gaol. It is said that Tilghman offered to allow Doolin a choice when they returned to Oklahoma Territory. If Doolin gave his word not to attempt to escape, he would not be handcuffed when his son saw him get down from the train. Doolin agreed to this and kept his word.

When they arrived at Arkansas City, Marshal Nix was there to meet them. Nix, together with other deputies, took Doolin to Guthrie and placed him in a federal gaol. In August Doolin somehow escaped from the federal gaol and went on the run. As was the practice in those days, any reward money that was offered for outlaws was payable to the person who caught him, and this applied to lawmen as well as civilians. In the case of Doolin, the reward poster offered $5,000 for the 'Capture and Conviction' of Bill Doolin, but despite having tracked the outlaw for nearly three years, Bill Tilghman never received a penny. Doolin was later shot and killed by Deputy US Marshal Heck Thomas.

The three law officers continued to search for the rest of the Doolin gang and eventually captured or killed them.

Bill Tilghman was appointed sheriff of Lincoln County at the beginning of 1900, during which time he was instrumental in suppressing the Ku Klux Klan and the 'Crazy Snake' Indian uprisings. In 1910 he was appointed chief of police of Oklahoma City, a post he held for two years. He went into retirement for the next 10 years, running his stock farm. Then in 1924, in response to a desperate plea from Governor Trapp, he was asked to go to a town called Cromwell and take control of law and order as town marshal.

Cromwell was a town that was deemed to be the 'wickedest' town in Oklahoma and was almost lawless. When Tilghman arrived over 50 per cent of the buildings in the town were either gambling halls, drinking saloons or brothels. Murder was common, and some bodies were known to have lain on the streets for days before being removed. Naked prostitutes stood in doorways or sat in windows, and drugs, rather than alcohol, were the main cause for concern.

Bill Tilghman and Charles F. Myton, seen here in Washington DC.

Outside the town oil derricks and storage tanks were the main source of revenue for the town and the men who worked there ran riot in the evenings and at weekends. The stench of oil permeated the town and hung heavy in the air. Nearly all the buildings were made of wood and they were sticky with oil residue.

With almost no help from the local sheriff, who was thought to be in the pay of the crime bosses who ran the town, Bill Tilghman started to make his presence felt. Slowly but surely he began to make a difference. Then one night, Tilghman, his deputy Hugh Sawyer and a local businessman were having a coffee when a shot rang out. Tilghman went to investigate and found the local federal Prohibition Agent Wiley Lynn, drunk and waving a gun about. Tilghman grasped Lynn's gun hand and tried to disarm him, but the gun went off. Bill Tilghman slumped against the wall of one of the wooden shacks that made up the town and died. He was 70 years old.

Tilghman's body lay in state in Oklahoma City before being buried, a mark of the respect felt for the man. One month later, almost every gambling house, saloon and brothel in Cromwell was torched, the fire being accelerated by the fact that the wooden buildings were coated with an oil residue, but not one private home was damaged. No one knows who or what caused the fires, but it is thought that one of Bill Tilghman's law enforcement friends, Chris Madsen, may have had a hand in exacting retribution for the murder of his friend and colleague.

Chapter 8

Chris Madsen

One of Bill Tilghman's closest friends was Deputy US Marshal Chris Madsen, who was born in Copenhagen, Denmark, in 1851 and had served first in the Danish army and then in the French Foreign Legion in Algiers. On being wounded during a battle in the Sudan he was honourably discharged. Still looking for excitement, he joined the French resistance movement in their struggle against the Prussians, but after France's defeat, he left to go to America.

On his arrival in New York in 1876, he enlisted in the 7th Cavalry and was posted out west to join General Armstrong Custer. While in transit his unit was transferred to the 5th Cavalry at Fort Hays and it was this that saved his life. Had he joined Custer and his men, he would have been involved in the Battle of the Little Big Horn and more than likely would have been killed.

For the next five years Madsen fought the Indians in their battle for their homeland and earned a mere $29 per month. Then in 1890 William Grimes was appointed US Marshal for the territory of Oklahoma and told to assign his own deputies. Recruiting men for such a dangerous and onerous task proved to be extremely difficult, so in desperation he turned to the

Chris Madsen.

32

army. On a visit to Fort Hays he asked the commanding officer to help and one name that was immediately suggested was that of Chris Madsen. Initially Madsen was reluctant to take the post, until he heard that the pay for a Deputy US Marshal was $250 a month, almost ten times what he was getting in the army. He accepted readily, and on 21 January 1891 was sworn in.

Madsen was joined by two other famous lawmen, Bill Tilghman and Henry (Heck) Thomas. The trio soon made their presence felt, especially among the whisky peddlers that were supplying the Indians. At one time Madsen was sent to transfer a notorious and violent horse-thief from the city gaol in Oklahoma to the federal gaol at Guthrie. The expected violence did not materialise and the man, known as the 'Dutchman', was safely moved. Two days later the man escaped and was later apprehended in a store in the town of Norman, stealing supplies. The officer who surprised him shot him in the stomach,

Deputy US Marshal Chris Madsen.

but the 'Dutchman' escaped once again, although this time he was wounded. Madsen was sent to track him down and return him to Guthrie to face trial. He found the 'Dutchman' on the banks of the South Canadian River, dying. Madsen returned the body to Guthrie and closed the case.

Chris Madsen was not only a fearless lawman, but also very astute and perceptive. Called to Fort Sill, where a murder had just taken place, he found that a man by the name of Pete Schneider had stabbed a man to death for smashing his accordion. The man, who was drunk, had taken exception to Schneider's playing of the accordion and had deliberately smashed it. Schneider then obtained a butcher's knife and stabbed the drunk several times in a fit of rage.

Chris Madsen knew Schneider as an Austrian with whom he had served as a soldier in the French Foreign Legion. Schneider had gone by the time Madsen arrived at Fort Sill, with no indication as to his whereabouts. Chris Madsen guessed that he would try to leave the country and so headed for the port of San Francisco. Within a day of arriving, Schneider turned up looking for passage to Europe and was arrested. Madsen's intuition had proved to be right.

Schneider was taken back to Oklahoma and tried for murder. On being convicted he was sentenced to life imprisonment in Alcatraz.

When a law officer was killed for passing on information regarding two criminals who were committing crimes around the town of Anadarko, Oklahoma, Chris Madsen took a personal interest. The officer concerned had been a former outlaw by the name of Jim Bourland, who had been captured by Madsen after committing a train hold-up. He had served his sentence and settled down just outside Anadarko, where he became a deputy sheriff. The two men, Tom Foster and Kid Lewis, went to Bourland's home one evening and shot him as he came out of his house.

Chris Madsen quickly formed a posse, and the trail led to them to Wichita Falls, where the pair were caught in the act of robbing the local bank. A gunfight ensued in which the two robbers killed the president of the bank and one of his cashiers. The pair were captured and taken

Rough Riders on top of San Juan Hill.

Above left: A double lynching.

Above right: Danish-born Deputy US Marshal Chris Madsen when one of Roosevelt's Rough Riders.

Right: A relaxed-looking Heck Thomas.

to the local gaol and placed in the care of the local sheriff. The posse was returning to El Reno, and was about an hour out of town, when a rider appeared asking them to return. The posse headed back to Wichita Falls, where, on their arrival, they were met with the sight of the two robbers hanging from a tree. The local people had decided on local justice without the need for a trial.

In 1897, Chris Madsen was transferred to the marshal's office in Kansas, but the climate in the area affected his wife's health and so they returned to El Reno, Oklahoma. Within months of his return, his wife had died and he was left to bring up his two children. Now out of a job, he was suddenly asked to help Colonel 'Teddy' Roosevelt form what was to become the 'Rough Riders'. In April 1898 he left his children in the care of friends and went to San Antonio and into the Spanish-American War.

When the war finally ended in August 1898, Chris Madsen returned to El Reno and was not immediately recognised by his children or his

Some of the Deputy US Marshals of the Western Circuit under Judge Isaac Parker. Seated: Chris Madsen, William Grimes and the Hitchcock girls. Standing: Heck Thomas, a gaoler, unknown, Tillman Dilly and Chief Clerk Warren Cleaver.

friends. While in action he had contracted a severe fever and lost over five stone in weight. Retiring to his small farm, he slowly regained his health and once again entered law enforcement when he was appointed Deputy US Marshal in Ardmore.

After John L. 'Jack' Abernathy became US Marshal of Oklahoma Territory in February 1906, Chris Madsen was appointed his chief deputy. When John Abernathy was removed from his position, Chris Madsen became the interim US Marshal from 1 January to 31 March 1911. After leaving active law enforcement in 1913, Madsen worked first as a guard, then a court bailiff, and as a superintendent at the Union Soldiers' Home.

Madsen had a long career as a Deputy US Marshal; however, he and various writers greatly inflated his reputation as a 'terror to evil doers'. Rarely involved in any gunfights, he spent most of his service in administrative work. On 9 January 1944, at age 92, Madsen died in the Masonic Home for the Aged in Guthrie while recovering from a broken hip. He was buried in Yukon, Oklahoma.

With the advent of newspapers and books, the West was becoming a place where the exploits of lawmen, gunfighters and outlaws were turned into folklore, and numerous accounts of marshals and sheriffs taming lawless towns abounded. Some of these men, and indeed women, were to have their exploits enhanced almost to the level of fantasy, and heroes were made out of men who were nothing more than cold-blooded killers.

Around this time, towns were springing up all over the United States and slowly but surely law and order were being introduced. Small towns had sheriffs and deputy sheriffs, while larger towns introduced the position of town marshal. This is not to be confused with the position of US Marshal, as happened in many books and magazines depicting the gunfighters and lawmen of the day. For example, Ben Thompson was one of the most feared gunmen around in the 1870s, and stories tell of him being the marshal of Austin, Texas. In this case this meant he was a city marshal, not a US Marshal.

Chapter 9

Ben Thompson

Ben Thompson was an immigrant from England. Born in the small industrial town of Knottingley, Yorkshire, his family emigrated to America when he was a small boy. He became a professional gambler, gunfighter and mercenary, before finally becoming a lawman.

Ben Thompson arrived in Austin, Texas, in early 1851 when he was just eight years old, and the sight that greeted the Thompson family was not an impressive one. The town, as it was then, consisted of a few wooden shacks spread over a dozen or so muddy acres. There were a couple of brick-built buildings, but predominantly the remainder were built out of timber.

Over the next decade the town expanded rapidly and the population increased to over 3,500. With the increase of people came an increase

in gambling, saloons, brothels and dance halls. It soon became obvious that the handful of law officers that were employed in the town were unable to cope with the increased crime that these various new attractions brought with them. This forced the town elders to form a vigilance committee in an effort to reduce the crime rate.

Head and shoulders shot of Ben Thompson when city marshal of Abilene, Texas.

Thompson started work as a trainee printer when he was 13 years old, but soon tired of this. In 1859 he had his first brush with the law when, after an argument with another boy regarding his shooting ability, he blasted the boy in the backside with a shotgun, for which he received 60 days in prison.

Shortly after his release he was travelling to New Orleans when he was involved in a knife fight with a Frenchman over a young lady. It appears that the Frenchman was making unwelcome advances to the young lady and Ben Thompson intervened on her behalf. The Frenchman was killed in the fight, but Thompson was not charged with anything as it was decided that he had acted in self-defence.

On his return to Austin the following year, Thompson enlisted in a battalion of veteran Indian fighters under the command of Captain Edward Burleson Jnr. Then the outbreak of the Civil War caused the whole of the area to be thrust into turmoil, as large numbers of men rallied to the Confederate cause and went to war. Ben Thompson joined the Confederate Second Texas Mounted Rifles and was involved in numerous battles, including the Battle of Galveston in 1863, where he was wounded. Throughout the war Thompson fought on the side of the Confederacy until its surrender and on his return home he married Catherine Moore, the daughter of a very successful landowner and merchant.

At the end of the war survivors of the Confederacy returned to Austin only to find that the city, as it had become, was under federal law enforced by Union troops. Federal law had now replaced southern law, and this was never made more apparent than when two black men were sworn in as police officers in Austin.

In 1865 Ben Thompson had his second brush with the law, when he shot and killed a drunken man who had threatened him with a shotgun. He was arrested and thrown into prison by the federal army. Realising that he was unlikely to get any justice

A dapper-looking Ben Thompson.

39

from the Unionists, he bribed two of the guards to let him out so that he could visit his family. Instead he headed for Mexico and fought on the side of Emperor Maximilian as a mercenary for two years. When Maximilian was captured, tried and executed, Ben Thompson left and returned to Texas.

On his return home he was involved in shooting his brother-in-law after the latter had struck Ben Thompson's wife with the butt of a gun. Ben Thompson had wounded his brother-in-law, but was arrested and charged with assault with intent to commit murder. He was found guilty by a military tribunal and sentenced to four years' hard labour. He was released after serving two years of his sentence after it was discovered that he had been tried illegally.

In 1873 he found himself in trouble with the law once again, this time in Ellsworth, Kansas. Ben, with his brother Billy, got work in a saloon as a house gambler, and when Ben got into an argument with two customers over money from a game, Billy, who had been drinking, intervened. The sheriff, Chauncey B. Whitney, was called and during the argument that ensued, Billy shot and killed him. Whitney had been unarmed and, being a friend of the Thompson brothers, had been trying to mediate. Ben, with the assistance of some other Texans, managed to get his brother out of the state. Billy Thompson was arrested three years later on a ranch outside Austin and taken back to Ellsworth to stand trial. A jury found him not guilty.

During the next few years Ben Thompson hired himself and his gun to the highest bidder and at one time joined up with Bat Masterson in protecting the Santa Fe Railroad against the Denver and Rio Grande Railroad over a dispute about the Royal George passage. When sober Ben Thompson was known for his honesty and generosity, but occasionally, when worse the wear from drink, he was a violent and deadly gunfighter.

When federal rule finally passed to Texas, and Austin City council

Chauncey B. Whitney.

40

started to govern itself, a city marshal was appointed to enforce the law. Draconian city laws were passed in an effort to control the transient population: for example, fishing with a pole was acceptable, but not with a net or trap. Horse racing was banned on Sundays, as was baseball, beating a drum, swimming or bathing in the Colorado River, which ran through the city. Houses of 'ill repute' were closed down, but within a year were flourishing again, as the majority of the property owners were on the city council. It was into this environment that Ben Thompson applied to become city marshal.

When he was appointed in December 1880, Thompson had lived intermittently in Austin while it had grown from a small town to a city. Many of the houses had indoor plumbing, there were gas streetlights and the railroad had reached it. The increased civilisation brought new laws and city ordinances, and in Austin in 1870 it was forbidden for anyone to carry a pistol, Bowie knife, brass knuckle-dusters, dagger or swordstick. The law was strictly enforced and anyone contravening the orders was punished quickly and severely.

One of Thompson's first notable arrests was that of another law officer, Sheriff James M. Brown of Lee County, Texas. Brown was one of the most feared sheriffs in the state and was not averse to using violence when it suited him. He had been travelling with a prisoner and a woman by the name of Mrs Amelia Schooman, and had entered

Austin with the intention of taking the train to Lee County. Sheriff Brown was wearing his gun, and Mrs Schooman, who was dressed as a man, was also carrying a gun, and this was against two of the city's ordinances. Thompson arrested both and had them brought before the mayor, who fined them for carrying guns within the city limits, and also fined Mrs Schooman for being inappropriately dressed by wearing men's clothes. The prisoner was put in the local gaol to await the arrival of the Deputy US Marshal.

Another arrest, which enhanced Ben Thompson's reputation, was when one of the most feared gunmen in Texas, John Ringo, arrived in Austin. Early on a Sunday morning,

Three-quarter shot of City Marshal Ben Thompson of Abilene, Texas.

after spending the night with one of the saloon ladies, Ringo discovered that his purse was missing and immediately confronted three local boys by waving his pistol in their faces, accusing them of stealing it. On finding nothing on them Ringo let them go, but the three boys went to the marshal's office and complained to Ben Thompson. Thompson immediately went to the hotel, and knowing of Ringo's reputation with a gun, kicked open the door of his room without knocking and arrested a very surprised John Ringo. Ringo was later fined $25 for carrying a pistol and a further $5 for disturbing the peace. He left the same day and never returned.

However, fame caught up with Ben Thompson when a man by the name of Jack Harris, who had been festering over an old gambling feud with Thompson for 18 years, arrived in Austin. On Tuesday 11 July 1882, he confronted Ben Thompson outside the vaudeville theatre in Austin and provoked him into drawing his gun. Thompson, with a number of years of experience as both gunfighter and lawman, was infinitely faster and more accurate, and seconds later Harris was dead. Thompson was arrested and charged with murder, despite claiming self-defence. He remained in custody for the next seven months before he came to trial and was subsequently acquitted.

Ben Thompson never returned to the office of city marshal, but went back to being a gambler and hired gun. Then, on 11 March 1884, Thompson was invited to go to the vaudeville theatre in Alamo City, Texas, by another lawman called John King Fisher – who was also a well-known gunfighter. Word had reached the city that the two men were arriving, and within minutes of reaching the theatre, both were dead -- each shot from behind by unseen assailants.

A casual-looking Ben Thompson.

Chapter 10

John King Fisher

John King Fisher was one of those lawmen that rode on both sides of the law. Born in Texas, Fisher was a bright lad who soon found himself mixing in the wrong company. He had begun by buying wild horses, which he tamed and sold at a profit, but then a number of stolen horses came his way and that's when his troubled career started. He was sentenced to two years in the state penitentiary, but served just the one because of his age.

He moved to the southern tip of Texas on his release, where he obtained work breaking horses. This is where he learned to shoot and handle a variety of other weapons. He became a very flamboyant character, wearing a sombrero festooned with gold braid, silk shirts, chaps made from the skin of a Bengal tiger, and a pair of silver-plated pistols with ivory grips, carried in silver-mounted holsters. A pair of silver spurs finished the outfit.

He joined a band of Mexican rustlers, but ended up shooting three of them after a disagreement over money. Slowly but surely his charismatic presence and ruthlessness helped him take over the gang, and he also organised two other gangs

John King Fisher.

John King Fisher with one of the members of his gang.

that operated either side of the border. At one time over 100 men were working for him.

John King Fisher bought a large ranch near Eagle Pass, Maverick County, Texas and used the ranch as his headquarters for operating his gangs. He organised deals with other Mexican bandits, who brought him stolen Mexican cattle in exchange for stolen Texas cattle.

Fisher had earned himself a reputation as a gunfighter and it is known that he killed at least seven men in minor disagreements. He was charged with murder on a number of occasions, but when brought to trial was never convicted.

In 1882 he became deputy sheriff of Uvalde County, Texas, and the following year was acting sheriff. While sheriff, he investigated a stagecoach robbery and trailed the two men concerned, Jim and Tom Hannehan, to their ranch near Leakey, Texas. When he challenged them they started firing at him and Tom Hannehan was killed. His brother surrendered himself and the robbery proceeds. John King Fisher, despite being a rather suspect character, showed that he took his position seriously.

While in Austin on business in 1884, he met an old friend and fellow gunfighter and former marshal, Ben Thompson. They had both been drinking heavily when they boarded a train to San Antonio. Unknown to John King Fisher, the last place Ben Thompson needed to go to was San Antonio, because of a long-standing feud that existed between him and Jack Harris and Joe Foster, who owned a gambling hall and vaudeville theatre in the city.

The two men went to the theatre on arrival in the city and Thompson demanded to see Joe Foster, saying he wanted to put an end to the feud between them. The two men went upstairs to the balcony where Foster and Harris were waiting, together with two other men. Foster refused to talk to Thompson, when suddenly the two men beside Foster and Harris stepped back. Realising that something was going to happen, both Ben Thompson and John King Fisher went for their guns, but before they could draw them a fusillade of shots rang out and the two men fell to the floor.

The two men with Harris and Foster then stepped forward and fired point blank into the head and body of both Fisher and Thompson. Thompson was said to have over 10 bullets in his body and Fisher 13 in his head and body. An investigation was carried out by the local police, but such was the reputation of both men, that very little interest was expressed in attempting to find those who actually pulled the trigger on them.

Chapter 11

Frank Dalton

The fragile nature of the office of marshal and sheriff was never more apparent than when applied to the Dalton brothers. One of them, Frank Dalton, was a Deputy US Marshal working under the famous 'Hanging Judge', federal Judge Isaac Parker, out of Fort Smith. There were numerous incidents of lawlessness, and one particular brutal incident happened in Arkansas at the end of November 1887, when two deputy marshals, Frank Dalton and James Cole, left Fort Smith to arrest David Smith for 'peddling whisky' to Indians. They were to arrest him on a warrant signed by Parker and were to bring him before his court.

Smith was living in a tent deep in Indian Territory, an area well known for its lawlessness. On seeing the two deputies approaching, Smith rushed out of his tent firing his revolver, the first shot hitting Frank Dalton in the chest and knocking him from his horse. James Cole immediately drew his weapon and shot Smith dead, but then two other men and a woman emerged from the tent firing their weapons. Cole fought back and killed one of the men and the woman before he was hit in the chest. Retiring to a safe distance to reload his

Frank Dalton.

weapon and tend to his own wound, he witnessed the remaining gang member, William Trawley, shoot Frank Dalton, first in the mouth and then in the head, as he lay dying on the ground. Cole, although badly hurt, managed to get back to Fort Smith to get help. Trawley was later captured and brought before Judge Isaac Parker, who sentenced him to be hanged for the murder of US Deputy Marshal Frank Dalton and other crimes. The sentence was duly carried out.

Four of Frank Dalton's brothers, Bill, Bob, Emmett and Grat, were on the other side of the law and carried out a succession of bank and train robberies before being gunned down during an attempted bank raid in Coffeyville, Kansas. Two of them, Bob and Grat, had served briefly as deputy town marshals in the Indian Territories before being sacked for dishonesty. It was then that they had decided that robbing banks and trains was infinitely more lucrative and less dangerous.

One survivor of the Coffeyville raid was Emmett Dalton, and he was sentenced to life imprisonment in the Kansas State Penitentiary at Lansing. After serving 14 years he was released and died in California in 1937.

Chapter 12

Commodore Perry Owens

Commodore Perry Owens was born on 29 July 1852. His father, Oliver H. Perry Owens, was named after Commodore Oliver Hazard Perry, a United States naval hero of the war of 1812. Commodore Perry Owens was born on a farm in Hawkind County, Tennessee and when he was a young boy, his family moved to Liberty Township, Hendrick County, Indiana, where they took up farming again. His father was an abusive, violent man, so it wasn't long before Commodore decided that this wasn't the life he wanted. At the age of 13 he ran away from home and headed into the Indian Territories. Nothing much is known about him during his early teen years, other than he was involved with some other young lads in whisky running, rustling and other minor criminal activities. Then in his late teens or early twenties he appears to have hired on as a buffalo hunter for the railroad. The killing of buffaloes each day to feed

the railroad workers highlighted his skill with a rifle and showed that he was an incredible shot. He was able to shoot a rifle accurately from the hip, without using the sights. After a few years of killing buffaloes, Commodore Owens moved on and found work on ranches in Oklahoma and New Mexico as a cowboy.

By the time he reached his 21st birthday, Commodore Owens had

Head and shoulders shot of Commodore Perry Owens.

settled down to work on the Hillard Roger's ranch outside Bartlesville, Oklahoma. At the beginning of 1881, Owens, now 28, was working as a ranch foreman for James D. Houck and A.E. Hennings in Navajo Springs, Arizona, northeast of present-day Holbrook, Arizona. Stories have arisen about Owens' dealings with the Navajo in the area during this period. It was their traditional territory, and they fiercely objected to settlers coming in and taking their lands. In one incident, when attacked by Navajo Indians who were trying to steal horses from a stage line post, Owens allegedly killed at least two of the Indians, and earned the nickname 'Iron Man'.

Commodore Perry Owens' first serious encounter with the law was in September 1883, when he was arrested by US Indian Agent Denis Matthew Riordan for the murder of a young Navajo boy near the Houck's ranch. Commodore Owens claimed that the young Indian boy was in the process of trying to rustle horses belonging to the ranch. When challenged, Owens said that the boy opened fire and that he had returned fire, his shot killing the youth. Owens was tried and subsequently acquitted of the murder by an Apache County jury.

Commodore Perry Owens was 5ft 10in tall, which was above average for that time. He had blue eyes that seemed to penetrate anyone he looked at. His most striking feature was his long red hair that cascaded halfway to his waist. He always carried two revolvers with the butts forward for the cross-draw, which he could draw with either right or left hand with incredible speed. There were many stories about his prowess with a gun and he had been seen standing 20ft from an empty tomato can and keeping it rolling with alternate shots from his two guns, until it was torn to pieces. Commodore Owens was a very private man, which some regarded as one of his greater attributes, together with his reputation for honesty and nerve. He was not the sociable type, but was reputed to have had an eye for the ladies.

Owens dressed as a typical cowboy, as seen in his photo taken in New Mexico. He wore his hair long in his youth, often curling it up

Commodore Perry Owens.

underneath his hat, and was often teased because of his unusual name. Around this time, he homesteaded outside Navajo Springs, building a small dugout/cabin, a well, and stables for his livestock near the stage station. He raised purebred horses. Owens is said to have named his place the 'Z-Bar Ranch', but this brand was not officially registered with the Apache County Recorder's Office.

Commodore Perry Owens' reputation as a gunfighter had preceded him and because of this he was nominated by the People's Party for sheriff of Apache County, Arizona. The Apache County Stockgrowers' Association, the Mormons and Mexicans supported him and in November 1885 he was appointed. His jurisdiction covered 21,177 square miles of territory, more than the combined area of New Hampshire and Vermont. (Ten years later Apache County was split into two counties, with the western part becoming Navajo County.)

A newspaper article after the election said, 'Mr. Owens is a well-liked, quiet, unassuming man, strictly honourable and upright in his dealings with all men.' Upon taking office in January 1887, Owens was presented with 14 bench warrants that had not been served by his predecessor, Jon 'Don' Lorenzo Hubbell. Included among these were warrants for the Mormon gunman Lot Smith, former Tombstone outlaw Ike Clanton, and rustler Andrew Arnold Cooper, an alias for Andy Blevins. The Clanton Gang and Blevins Brothers both had notorious reputations in Arizona as rustlers and outlaws. Citizens of Apache County expected the new sheriff to take action against the two gangs. One of his first tasks was to clean up the filthy gaol and carry out essential repairs to the dilapidated building and account for public funds down to the postage stamps that had been used.

One of the first warrants on the list that he had been given was that of Ike Clanton. The Clantons had a ranch east of Tombstone and were known to be cattle rustlers and smugglers. They would steal cattle, re-brand them and take them across the border into Mexico to sell. Mexican soldiers had killed old man Clanton some years ago after being caught in the act of taking stolen cattle into Mexico. His sons, however, kept up the family 'tradition' of rustling cattle and stealing. They had also been long-time enemies of the Earp brothers, which resulted in the now famous 'Gunfight at the OK Corral' on 26 October 1881, which is covered later. Ike Clanton had fled the scene as soon as the shooting started, while his younger brother died in the shootout. Ike Clanton moved north, away from Tombstone, to Apache County, east of Springerville, where he continued to ply his trade, having said that ranching was 'very profitable when you didn't have to buy the cows.'

The Clanton gang now became the biggest threat to law and order in Apache County. Things came to a head when, on 6 November 1886, a rancher by the name of Isaac Ellinger was shot at Clanton's ranch by gang member Lee Renfo. Ellinger had gone to the ranch to confront Ike Clanton over some of his stolen cattle. A witness, who was with Ellinger, said it was entirely unprovoked, and Ellinger died of his wounds four days later. On Christmas Day 1886 another Clanton gang member, Billy Evans, shot and killed Jim Hale (who had identified cattle stolen by the Clantons) in cold blood. When Owens first became sheriff he hired ex-Texas lawman Jeff Milton as a deputy and sent him to arrest the Clantons, but such was the threat of violence that Milton later backed out.

A young Ike Clanton.

In May 1886 the Apache County grand jury again indicted Ike Clanton and other gang members for rustling and smuggling. Sheriff Owens sent deputies Rawhide Jake Brighton and Albert Miller to go and arrest Ike Clanton and his associates (Brighton was also a Springerville constable and a range detective or 'secret service officer' hired by the cattlemen's association). Ike Clanton was not at his ranch, but luck was on the side of the deputies and they ran into Ike Clanton while on the trail on 1 June 1887. The moment Ike Clanton saw the two deputies he knew he was in trouble and pulled his Winchester from its holster. He turned his horse toward a clump of trees looking for cover. Jake Brighton had recognised Clanton the moment he saw him and pulled his Winchester and fired, hitting Clanton's saddle horn. Before he could return fire, Jake Brighton's second shot was more accurate and Ike Clanton fell from his horse dead. In July, two more gang members, Billy Evans and Longhair Sprague, were killed when ranchers trailing stolen horses shot the rustlers dead in a gunfight. Then Rawhide Jake Brighton killed another gang member, Lee Renfo, when Renfo went for his gun as Brighton tried to arrest him. The remaining members of the gang disappeared and the murderous reign of the Clanton gang was at an end.

Another name on the list of warrants was that of Andy Blevins, a native of Mason County, Texas, west of Austin. Blevins had come to Arizona in 1885 with his brother Charlie, in order to escape arrest for

51

crimes he was said to have committed in Texas, which included murder. In an effort to avoid arrest, Andy Blevins changed his name to Cooper. After settling in, the Blevins brothers were eventually joined by their younger brothers, their mother, and the remainder of the Blevins clan. Within months the Blevins were involved in rustling and Andy Blevins was known to have killed three Navajo men after he was seen rustling a herd of horses from the Navajo reservation. There were also rumours that he had killed two lawmen who were tracking him. Cooper's two half-brothers, John Black and William 'Hamp' Hampton, had joined the family and were also suspected cattle rustlers.

During this period, a range war had erupted in Yavapi County between the Graham and Tewksbury families, which was to become known as the Pleasant Valley War. Cooper/Andy Blevins and his brothers became allies of the Graham family, who were essentially cattlemen. They had started feuding with the Tewksbury family, who had also been cattle ranchers, after the latter had introduced herds of sheep onto their land. The Tewksbury family was part Indian, and it is thought that racial prejudice may have been one of the underlying causes for the feuding. Although the feud occasionally spilled over into his county, Commodore Owens seems to have remained neutral.

The problem started in 1887, when the Texas-based Aztec Land and Cattle Company bought the Hashknife brand from the Continental Cattle Company, bringing some 33,000 head of cattle and 2,000 horses

Posse of Hashknife cowboys.

Hashknife cowboy.

into Arizona. With the herd came the Hashknife cowboys, most of whom were hard-working, hard-drinking, fun-loving men, but among them were a small number of troublemakers and outlaws whose only aim was to cause as much trouble as they could when in town. Some of them were wanted men and had been linked to two train robberies at Canyon Diablo. Initially local towns of Holbrook, Springerville and St Johns welcomed the men and their money, but they soon became disillusioned after clearing up the aftermath of their riotous behaviour, their excessive drinking and shooting up the towns.

The situation turned from a problem into a war when the Daggs brothers of Flagstaff, the largest sheep owners in northern Arizona, drove a herd of 1,500 sheep toward Pleasant Valley. The Tewksburys, who had had a falling-out with Tom Graham, the cattle king of the valley, had invited them in. When news of the impending invasion of sheep spread among the cattlemen, a line had been drawn at the Tonto Rim: no sheep in Pleasant Valley. As the Daggs' sheep edged closer and closer to the line, a cowboy galloped up to the Graham Ranch with the news that 'Woollies were swarming down the trail into Pleasant Valley.' The drovers were John, Jim and Ed Tewksbury and their associate Bill Jacobs. The Pleasant Valley War had begun.

The Daggs brothers were extremely well connected both politically and legally and had judges, lawmen and politicians among their close friends.

Pleasant Valley.

In February 1887 a Navajo Indian working for the Tewksburys was herding sheep in an area called the Mongollon Rim, which had been accepted as the line across which sheep were not permitted, when he was ambushed, shot and killed by Tom Graham. Graham then beheaded the corpse and buried it where the worker fell. In August 1887 Mart Blevins, the head of the Blevins family, went out to search for some missing horses after suspecting the Tewksburys were behind the theft. He never returned, and his horse and rifle were recovered near the Tewksbury ranch. The Blevins boys, consisting of Andy, Charlie and some of their ranch hands, rode out in search of their father in the Tewksbury territory. The three brothers split up and Charlie went to the Hashknife camp, where ranch hands John Payne, Thomas Carrington and Robert Glaspie joined him. Along the way, Tom Tucker, a sworn enemy of the Tewksburys, joined them. They tracked down the Tewksburys to a sheep herder's ranch owned by George Newton. Hamp and his men asked Newton for some food, but they were met by Ed Tewksbury, who told them to go away in no uncertain terms. When they refused to, the Tewksburys drew their guns and a shootout occurred in which Charlie Blevins and John Payne were killed. When the Grahams came back to bury the bodies, they found the ranch burned to the ground, and the Tewksburys were nowhere to be seen.

The war continued and on 17 August 1887, William Graham was rounding up his family's horses when he was shot in the gut with a shotgun. The young man managed to ride back to his home, but his wound was so severe that when he arrived his intestines were hanging out of his

A poor-quality
photograph of
Hashknife cowboys
Billy Wilson and
Tom Tucker.

stomach. Just before he died he identified Ed Tewksbury as his murderer to
his brothers. However, the Apache County deputy sheriff said that James
D. Houck, who was a friend of the Tewksburys, had confessed that he was
the man who shot Willy Graham after mistaking him for his brother John
Graham. No one believed this, and it was thought that this was just a way
to keep the allegations away from Ed Tewksbury. A warrant was issued
for the arrest of Ed Tewksbury, but when lawmen came to arrest him for
the murder of the young William Graham, he had already fled to the hills.

In September 1887, the remaining Grahams rode to the Tewksbury
cabin in the early morning. They concealed themselves in the brush
surrounding the cabin and waited. Later that morning they spotted
John Tewksbury Jnr and William Jacobs come out on their horses.

The Grahams ambushed and killed both men. They then went to the cabin and started firing. As the battle continued, hogs began devouring the bodies of Tewksbury and Jacobs. According to some accounts, the Grahams did not offer a truce, but John Tewksbury's wife, Eva, came out of the cabin with a shovel. The firing stopped while she scooped out shallow graves for her husband and his companion. Firing on both sides resumed once she was back inside, but no further deaths occurred that day. After many hours of shooting from both sides, the Grahams left when they were warned that the law was approaching.

Over the next few years several lynchings and unsolved murders of members of both families took place, often committed by masked men. The elder John Tewksbury Snr died of natural causes. One of the Tewksburys' allies, George Newton, drowned mysteriously in the Salt River and many, including his family, thought that the Grahams were responsible. Both the Tewksburys and the Grahams continued fighting until there were only two left.

With all of his family gone, Tom Graham left Prescott and moved to the Salt River Valley. He settled in Tempe and married a minister's

Lynching of an unknown man during the Yavapi County Range War.

daughter named Annie Melton. On 2 August 1892, while delivering a load of wheat from a store, Tom Graham, the last of the Grahams involved in the feud, was fatally shot in the back by two assassins. The assassins called to him, and as Tom looked over his shoulder, a shot rang out. Just before he died, Tom Graham named Ed Tewksbury and John Rhodes as his attackers.

Ed Tewksbury was arrested and accused of the murder of Tom Graham. During the first trial the well-known Arizona attorney Thomas Fitch defended him, but that ended abruptly due to a legal technicality. During the trial, Tom Graham's widow, Annie, attempted to shoot Ed Tewksbury with a pistol, but it got caught in her dress, and she was promptly arrested and removed from the court. The jury in the second trial could not reach a verdict after more than 100 witnesses had been called, and many stated that Ed Tewksbury had been one of the murderers. The jury found him not guilty, as his defence was that at the time of the murder he was miles away in the town of Tempe and had witnesses to prove it. Edwin Tewksbury died in Globe, Arizona, in April 1904. On his deathbed he confessed that he did kill Tom Graham, and did so by having fresh horses along the route to Tempe, where witnesses saw him.

When old man Blevins disappeared in June 1887 it was thought that one of the Tewksbury faction might have killed him. The Blevins brothers searched for their father and in one of the incidents with the Tewksburys, Charlie Blevins and another were killed. Andy Blevins returned to Holbrook and was heard bragging about the killings.

Sheriff Owens had inherited an old warrant for Andy Cooper (Blevins)' arrest, but had never activated it. Some said it was because Owens and Blevins were friends, having been cowboys together. Others said Owens was afraid of Blevins, who was known as a fine shot and a cold killer, but what is more likely the truth is that as long as the Blevins gang stayed out of his county, Commodore Owens left them alone. The

Edwin Tewksbury, the last surviving member of the Tewksbury/Blevins feud.

57

warrant was for the theft of some 25 horses from a Mormon, who had tracked his horses to the Blevins Canyon Creek Ranch and identified Andy. An independent witness, a county official, had also seen Andy Blevins driving the horses.

Faced with no other option, on Sunday 4 September 1887 Sheriff Commodore Perry Owens heard that Andy Blevins/Cooper was in Holbrook and rode to the family house to serve on him the outstanding warrant for rustling. When Owens reached the house he was told that there were 12 people inside, including Cooper (the eldest Blevins brother), the younger brothers John and Sam Houston Blevins; the brothers' mother, Mrs Blevins; John Blevins' wife Eva and their infant son; a family friend, Miss Amanda Gladden; house guest Mose Roberts; and several children.

Sheriff Owens knocked on the door, cradling his Winchester rifle in his arm, and, when Andy Blevins answered with a pistol in hand, Owens told him to come out of the house, stating that he had a warrant

Commodore Perry Owens with two other sheriffs: St George Creaghe (sitting centre), Tom Perex (standing centre) Commodore Perry Owens (standing right centre).

for his arrest. Blevins refused to come out and tried to shut the door. Owens dropped the rifle to his hip and shot Blevins through the door, hitting him in the abdomen. On hearing the shot, Andy's half-brother, John Blevins, pushed his pistol out the door to Owens' right and fired a shot. He missed and killed Andy's saddle horse, which was tied to a tree. Owens turned toward his assailant and fired, wounding John Blevins in the arm, and putting him out of the fight.

In an attempt to see the three sides of the house, Owens backed away into the yard. Looking through a window Owens saw Andy Blevins staggering around inside. Realising that Andy Blevins was still a threat, Commodore Owens fired a third time through the front wall of the cottage, hitting Andy in the right hip. As this was going on, Mose Roberts, who had been visiting with the family, jumped out of a side window. Roberts saw the sheriff and immediately turned to run and as he did so Owens shot him, the bullet passing through his back and out of his chest. Roberts stumbled around the back of the house and fell at the back door. Later it was claimed that Mose Roberts was unarmed at the time, but a blood-covered pistol was recovered from by the back door where he fell. A doctor who attended the scene confirmed this to be true.

Tragically, after Owens shot Roberts, 15-year-old Samuel Houston Blevins ran out the front door, holding his brother Andy's Colt revolver, which he had taken from the mortally wounded outlaw. The younger brother yelled 'I'll get him.' His mother desperately tried to hold him back, but Sam broke loose. As the youth came towards him pointing the gun, Owens shot and killed him. Sam fell backward, dying in his mother's arms. The whole incident took less than one minute and the shootout further enhanced Commodore Owens' reputation.

Locally, Owens was praised for ridding the county of Andy Cooper/Blevins, a notorious outlaw, although some thought the shooting of the 15-year old boy unnecessary. Three separate coroner's juries found Owens' actions justifiable. The Gunfight at Holbrook, as it became known, grew to be legendary in most circles, but Owens' lack of formal education became a problem. As the county became more developed, the constituency began to wonder if Owens had the skills to be as good an administrator as he was a lawman.

The outlaws Robert W. 'Red' McNeil and Grant S. 'Kid' Swingle continued to frustrate Owens' attempts to capture them. Owens was unjustly criticized for holding John Blevins in custody, although he was pardoned by the governor for shooting at the sheriff during the conflict at his house. The days of the gun-toting sheriff were numbered and Commodore Perry Owens finished out his term as Apache County sheriff when he was defeated in the election of November 1888 by his former deputy, St George Creaghe.

In 1890, Commodore Perry Owens sought nomination once again for the office of Apache County sheriff, this time on the Democratic ticket. He was defeated by Joseph Woods, who was later defeated in the election by Republican W.R. Campbell. Owens went to work for Campbell as his chief deputy.

In August 1893, Owens was appointed to the position of Deputy US Marshal under William Kidder Meade. Two years later, in 1895, he was appointed sheriff of the newly created Navajo County by Governor Louis Cameron Hughes and served two years. Owens appointed as his under sheriff his nephew Robert Hufford, son of his sister Mary Francis.

At the end of his term as sheriff of Navajo County, Commodore Perry Owens did not seek re-election. He retired to Seligman, Arizona, where he bought property and opened a general store and a saloon. While the other buildings have long since been torn down, Owens' house still stands.

Owens married a woman named Elizabeth Jane Barrett in 1902. The couple had no children. The census of 1910 shows that Owens and his wife were residing in San Diego, California. Owens eventually returned to Seligman. Commodore Perry Owens died in 1917 aged 67 of Bright's disease and was buried in Flagstaff, Arizona.

Chapter 13

John Behan

One of those lawmen who carried out his duties with quiet efficiency and was able to maintain strict law and order was John Behan.

Born in Westport, Missouri, in 1845, John Behan started his employment as a freighter at Fort Lowell, but soon found the work to be tedious and unrewarding. In 1866 he took up the post of deputy sheriff of Yavapai County, and four years later became the sheriff. When the post of sheriff of Cochise County became available, John Behan took it, and with his reputation for being a brave and honest lawman, started to clean up the county. Not long after he had taken office, Virgil Earp became city marshal of Tombstone and immediately recruited two of his brothers, Wyatt and Morgan, as 'special deputies'.

John Behan had been living with a woman by the name of Josephine Sarah Marcus, who, after she had left Behan, married Wyatt Earp. Earp, jealous of Behan, wanted the job of sheriff of Cochise County and had decided to run against him in the next election. Their dislike of each other was further exacerbated by the fact that John Behan had arrested Doc Holliday, Wyatt Earp's friend, on suspicion of killing a stagecoach driver during an attempted hold-up.

Virgil Earp then arrested Frank Stilwell, one of Behan's deputies, for the murder. Both Holliday and Stilwell were eventually released for lack of evidence. It appears that both were being used as pawns in a game of

A young John Behan.

61

Above left: Frank Stilwell.

Above right: An innocent looking Frank Stilwell.

hate. In the meantime the Earps were involved in a conflict with the Clanton and McLaury families. Cattle that the families had sold in Tombstone were believed to have been stolen from a farm in Mexico. Wyatt Earp also believed that the Clantons had stolen one of his horses.

The Earps faced the Clanton and McLaurys in the now famous OK Corral incident. John Behan, realising that it was going to turn into a bloodbath, attempted to intervene, but was ignored. The Earps used their positions in the law to settle their personal score with the Clantons and McLaurys.

After the one-sided gunfight, details of which are in the section covering Wyatt Earp, John Behan immediately arrested the Earps and Holliday on suspicion of murder and placed them in gaol. They were all found not guilty after what can only be described as a sham trial, and were released.

Above left: John Behan.

Above right: Wanted poster put out by friends of the Clantons after the shootout at the OK Corral.

A disgusted John Behan returned to his normal duties and several years later became superintendent of the Yuma Territorial State Prison. Two years later he became a US federal agent in charge of trying to control the smuggling in the area. During the Boxer Rebellion in China, John Behan was a special agent for the US government assigned to China. He died peacefully in Tucson on 7 June 1912.

Chapter 14

William Milton Breakenridge

Among the infamous lawmen were a number of lesser-known ones, but their contribution to law and order was no less important. One of these was a quietly spoken man who gained the respect of all those who came up against him, without drawing his pistol. His name was William Milton Breakenridge.

Born on Christmas Day in 1846, at Watertown, Wisconsin, Billy Breakenridge, as he was known, ran away from home after being told he was too young to enlist in the Union army at the outbreak of the Civil War. Despite this he joined as a wagon boy with the quartermaster's department.

When the wagon train arrived at Rolls, Missouri, after a long and arduous journey, Billy Breakenridge took his wages and headed for

William Breakenridge.

Denver, Colorado, to see his elder brother. Over the next few years he had a number of jobs, then in 1868 he and his brother went looking for work and visited a number of famous towns. In Colorado he met Marshal Tom Smith, a meeting he never forgot.

In the summer of 1878, Billy Breakenridge found himself penniless and in the lawless town of Phoenix, Arizona. The local sheriff, Tom Broadway, offered him a job as deputy sheriff and it was around this time that a group called the Vigilante Committee became known. Their treatment of rustlers and law-breakers in general became legendary and very soon Phoenix became a quiet town.

Craving more excitement, Breakenridge headed for Tombstone. On the way he tried his hand at prospecting in the Dragoon Mountains, Cochise's stronghold, but with no success. He acquired a job in a lumber camp and on weekends went into Tombstone. It was while in Tombstone that he saw and met Wyatt and Morgan Earp, and the infamous Doc Holliday. He drank in the Bird Cage Saloon and was served drinks by the notorious 'Buckskin Frank' Leslie.

Then out of the blue, he was approached by Sheriff John Behan and offered the job of deputy sheriff. Most of his work at first was in the office, dealing with the paperwork and such like, but then an incident in the town of Galeyville changed all that. A professional gunfighter by the name of Johnny Ringo had lost all his money in a card game in a saloon, and so decided that he would relieve the miners he was playing with of their cash. His reputation for being the fastest gunman alive, not to mention his unstable character, prevented any of the miners objecting to him taking the money.

Above left: Morgan Earp.

Above right: Buckskin Frank Leslie.

Above left: Johnny Ringo.

Above right: Johnny Ringo.

The following morning, having sobered up, he realised what he had done and returned the money to the miners. However some of the miners had already reported the incident to the sheriff and Billy Breakenridge was told to serve the warrant for his arrest. At first Sheriff Behan thought that it might be better if Breakenridge was accompanied, but Billy refused this, thinking that there would be less hassle if he were alone.

Two days later, at a cabin just outside Galeyville, Breakenridge knocked on the door and it was opened by a bleary eyed Johnny Ringo. An apprehensive Breakenridge explained that he had a warrant for his arrest, to which Ringo replied that he had better come in and have some breakfast before they went.

Breakenridge allowed Ringo to keep his guns in case Apaches, who were known to be in the area, attacked them. They reached Tombstone the following night and the next day Ringo appeared in court before Judge Stillwell. Given his bail, Ringo left town for Galeyville, only to be accosted by two vigilantes, sent by Judge Stillwell, who tried to serve an arrest warrant on him once again. Ringo got the drop on them and took their guns, suspecting that the Earps were involved. Returning to Tombstone, Ringo went to Breakenridge and insisted that he be placed in custody so that he could appear in court the next day. The following day he appeared in court but the charges were dropped because of lack of evidence.

Some months later Breakenridge and another deputy were sent to investigate the hold-up of the Bisbee–Tombstone stagecoach. Robbers had stolen the express box and the mail. Descriptions given by the passengers identified the two men as Frank Stillwell and Ben Spence. The two were traced to Bisbee, arrested and returned to Tombstone. Virgil Earp, who was town marshal, told Breakenridge that the Clantons and McLaurys were out to get him for arresting their friends. Billy Breakenridge spoke to Tom McLaury, who denied all knowledge of the statement, making the point that he had no interest in either Stillwell or Spence.

Then a stagecoach was robbed and the two men involved parted when the posse went on their trail. One of the men, named McMasters, arrived in Tombstone and rumour had it that Virgil Earp warned him that a US Marshal was on his trail and supplied him with a stolen fresh horse. The following day Ike Clanton, for some unknown reason, told him that the stolen horse could be found at McLaury's ranch.

Breakenridge rode out to the McLaury ranch and asked for the return of the horse. He was told that it wasn't there, but it could be brought the following morning. He was invited to stay the night, and despite being in the presence of Curly Bill Brocius and his men, all of whom were known rustlers and gunmen, Breakenridge was respected and left alone.

The following morning, the horses were outside saddled up and ready to go. Frank McLaury warned Breakenridge that some of the outlaws wanted the horse and intended to ambush Billy on the trail. Billy watched his back and spotted three men in the distance moving towards him. Stopping at a lumber camp, he left his own horse with the men there and galloped away on the other horse. He easily outstripped his pursuers and rode into Tombstone. He later made arrangements to have his own horse returned to him.

Another stagecoach hold-up in March 1881 again threw suspicion on friends of the Earps and although one man was arrested, he somehow quickly escaped. The driver of the stage, Bud Philpot, and one of the passengers were killed in the ambush and some days later, Doc Holliday's girlfriend 'Big Nose' Kate, while in one of her regular drunken states, shouted to all and sundry that Doc Holliday had shot and killed Philpot. Sheriff John Behan promptly arrested him, but he was released on a $5,000 bail provided by Wyatt Earp. The bitterness between the Earps and Sheriff Behan had reached a new low. They each accused the other of being involved in the stagecoach robberies, and of using their positions to help cover up the fact.

Two days later, on 25 October, Ike Clanton and Tom McLaury came into town in their wagon to collect supplies. Ike Clanton went for a meal and was accosted by Doc Holliday, who accused him of badmouthing his friends the Earps, and warned him to keep his mouth shut or face the consequences. Ike Clanton, unlike his father and brother Billy, was not a gunfighter and was not going to go up against Doc Holliday.

The following morning, on 26 October, the famous 'Gunfight at the OK Corral', occurred, which is described elsewhere in the book.

The following year, in March 1882, Morgan Earp was killed while playing billiards with his brother Wyatt. Frank Stillwell and Pete Spence were charged with his murder, but Billy Breakenridge claimed that Frank Stillwell could not have done it, because he had been seen in Tucson the following morning and that was over 75 miles away.

But Wyatt Earp and his friends had other ideas, and killed Frank Stillwell in the railway yard at Tucson before he could defend himself against the accusations. They then left for Tombstone. The sheriff of Pima County wired Sheriff John Behan, calling for the arrest of Wyatt Earp and his friends for murder, but before the wire was received, Earp had left Tombstone.

 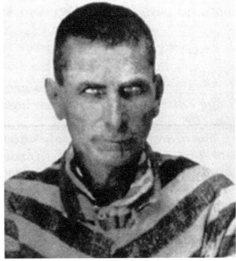

Above left: A young Morgan Earp just before he became sheriff.

Above right: Pete Spence, said to have been involved in the murder of Morgan Earp.

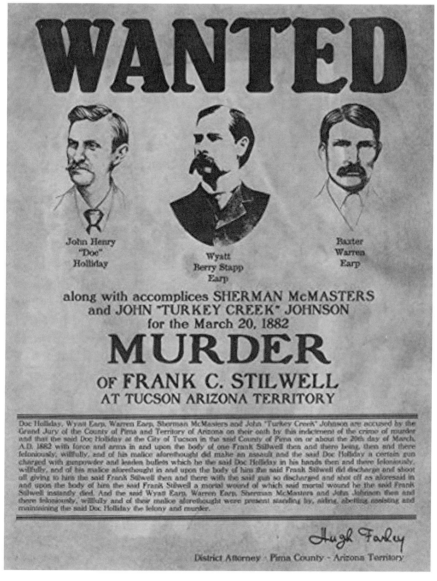

Wyatt Earp and Doc Holliday wanted poster.

One month later a robbery took place at the Tombstone Mining and Milling Company at Charleston and when one of the employees tried to stop the thieves he was shot down in cold blood. The two robbers made their way to a ranch near Antelope Springs, owned by Jack Chandler. Chandler was in town when they arrived at his place and the first he knew of them was when one of his men arrived with a note from them demanding money. Chandler passed the note over to the sheriff, who in turn passed it over to Billy Breakenridge, who immediately offered to go alone and try to persuade them to give themselves up. His offer was refused and a posse was quickly formed.

The posse headed out towards the ranch and, on stopping a little way outside, they hid their horses and quickly surrounded the ranch house. Before any dialogue could begin, two of the posse ran forward and hammered on the door, demanding that it be opened in the name of the sheriff. The door was flung open and shots rang out, and both members of the posse fell to the floor dead. With that a gunfight ensued. Billy Breakenridge was the only member of the posse not harmed in any way and the gunfight, which lasted less than a minute, left two men dead and three wounded. Both outlaws were wounded in the incident, but they were arrested and taken into custody. It is not known what happened to them.

At the beginning of 1883 Billy Breakenridge resigned and went into ranching for a year, but then sold out because the life was too mundane. He was appointed a Deputy US Marshal and then became special officer for the Southern Pacific Railroad, covering the territory between El Paso and Yuma. Until the day he retired Billy Breakenridge chased train robbers and outlaws through every kind of terrain imaginable, earning the respect of friend and foe alike.

He died in 1931 at his home in Tucson at the age of 85 leaving behind a legacy of law and order.

Chapter 15

Wyatt Earp

One of the most famous characters associated with the Wild West was Wyatt Earp. There have been numerous books, stories, interviews and films about the man and his life, almost all depicting him to having been a fearless and dedicated lawman – but nothing could be further from the truth.

Born in Montmouth, Illinois, in 1848, Wyatt Earp started his law enforcement career when he was appointed constable of Lamar, Missouri, but this didn't last long as he was arrested for horse theft. He escaped from custody and fled to Kansas, joining a team of buffalo hunters, and it was here that he honed his shooting skills.

Wyatt's brothers, Virgil and James were both married and living in Wichita, Kansas. However, both their wives were arrested on numerous occasions for prostitution and keeping bawdy houses. They all later moved to Tombstone to meet up with their other brother Morgan.

After a few years of living and working in the wilderness, Wyatt Earp moved to Wichita where he joined the local police force. Within months he had been fired after a fight with a fellow officer. He then moved to Dodge City and was appointed deputy city marshal under Marshal Charlie Bassett. It was here that he met and befriended the infamous gambler/gunfighter Doc Holliday. Wyatt Earp became involved in a confrontation with a large number of

Wyatt Earp when a deputy sheriff.

Above left: Virgil Earp.

Above right: James Earp.

Left: Louise Houston Earp, wife of Morgan Earp.

drunken cowboys, and Doc Holliday assisted him in arresting the ringleaders. This act cemented their friendship for many years.

Wyatt Earp left Wichita and headed towards Tombstone to meet with his brothers Virgil and Morgan and their wives. In September 1881 Virgil Earp was appointed city marshal of Tombstone and immediately recruited his two brothers as special deputies. Doc Holliday at this time had also appeared in Tombstone and became a fixture in the gambling saloons. Holliday, a former dentist suffering from consumption, had become a renowned gambler and gunfighter. He was not in the same class as Ben Thompson, Bat Masterson or Wild Bill Hickok, but nevertheless he was a very dangerous man to cross.

Tombstone in 1880.

It was in Tombstone that the famous 'Gunfight at the OK Corral' took place. This incident has been the subject of numerous books, articles and films, some of which have been completely inaccurate. The problem between the Earps and the Clanton and McLaury families had been festering for a long time, and when Ike Clanton got into a dispute with Doc Holliday, the Earps grasped the opportunity to settle the matter.

The next day, Wednesday 26 October 1881, Ike Clanton and Tom McLaury rode into town and were promptly arrested by Virgil Earp for carrying firearms within the city limits. On being disarmed and then released, the two men joined Billy Clanton and Frank McLaury at the OK Corral. Virgil Earp suddenly took it into his head to go and disarm both Billy Clanton and Frank McLaury, and called upon his brothers to go and help him. Doc Holliday, anxious for any excuse to get at Ike Clanton, also volunteered to go along even though Wyatt Earp told him it wasn't his fight.

Sheriff John Behan, who was in town at the time and realised there was going to be a bloodbath if something wasn't done, went to Billy Clanton and Frank McLaury and pleaded with them to give up their guns. They agreed, but only if the Earps and Holliday gave up their guns, and they knew that was never going to happen, because as law enforcement officers the Earps were entitled to carry guns. At 3pm the three Earp brothers and Doc Holliday, dressed almost identically in long black frontier coats and broad-rimmed black hats, marched side by side down Fourth Street, then into Fremont Street and towards the OK Corral – and into folklore. The gunfight actually took place in a vacant lot between two buildings and behind the OK Corral.

The two groups of men faced each other. Virgil Earp is said to have called out, 'You men are under arrest. Throw out your weapons and

Above: The OK Corral in Tombstone after the fire that ravaged the town.

Left: Doc Holliday.

Below: Tom McLaury, Frank McLaury and Billy Clanton lying in their coffins after being killed during the gunfight with the Earps at the OK Corral.

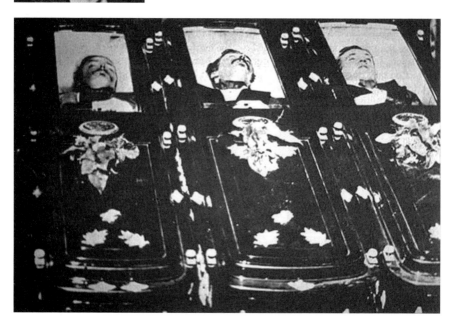

put up your hands'. Wyatt Earp always claimed that Frank McLaury went for his gun and the others, also reaching for their weapons, followed him. This appears to be a contradiction, as Tom McLaury, whom witnesses say was unarmed, was shot in the back by Doc Holliday and killed as he tried to run away. Billy Clayton was gunned down by both Morgan and Virgil Earp, but managed to get a shot into Virgil Earp's leg before falling to the ground dead. Billy Claiborne was shot and killed by Morgan Earp. The one-sided gunfight lasted between 20 and 30 seconds, but was later extended dramatically by writers and the cinema.

Ike Clanton was the only one to escape with his life. Sheriff Behan arrested the Earps and Holliday, and charged them with murder, but at their trial Judge Wells

Ike Clanton.

Spicer decided that their actions were justified and found them not guilty. No one appears to have listened to the witnesses, who included Sheriff John Behan, who said:

'Billy Clanton and Frank McLaury were the only ones armed and when Virgil Earp called out to them, Billy Clanton replied saying that they didn't want to fight and raised their hands, and still had their hands raised when Morgan Earp and Doc Holliday opened fire'.

Other witnesses who supported John Behan were not called to give evidence. The fact that the judge is said to have been related to the Earps also seems to have been overlooked by the law at the time.

From that moment on, law and order in Tombstone went steadily downhill. Morgan Earp was shot and killed while playing a game of billiards with Wyatt Earp, and Virgil Earp was seriously wounded and crippled in an attempted assassination some time later. Wyatt Earp left Tombstone and went to Arizona, where he was appointed a special deputy town marshal in Cochise County, after a sudden increase in lawlessness in the state. Wyatt Earp led a number of posses, hunting down 'criminals' during this period with such a disregard for the law itself, that the then President of the United States, Chester A. Arthur, threatened to impose martial law in the state of Arizona if the posses didn't stop.

Above left: Warren Earp.

Above right: Luke Short.

The posses were disbanded and Wyatt Earp, together with his brother Warren and Doc Holliday, headed for Colorado, looking for the men who were involved in the murder of his brother Morgan. They in turn were pursued by Sheriff Bob Paul with warrants for their arrest for murder. Paul caught up with the trio in Colorado and asked for their extradition, but it was refused and subsequently the charges were dropped. A number of reasons were put forward, among them that the Arizona courts had more cases than they could successfully handle, and another that Wyatt Earp still had powerful friends back in Tombstone.

Ike Clanton was killed some months later by Springville constable Jonah Brighton, after trying to escape when caught with some rustled cattle.

At the end of May 1883, Luke Short, a saloon and gambling-house owner, who was having trouble with what he described as a 'band of armed men', contacted Wyatt Earp. The men wanted to take over his business using political differences and business rivalry as an excuse to force him to leave town, claiming that if he returned he would be killed. Wyatt Earp called in some of his friends, Doc Holliday, Bat Masterson,

Above left: Abe Graham, also known as 'Shotgun Collins'.

Above right: Constable 'Prairie Dog' Dave Morrow of Dodge City.

Charlie Bassett, Shotgun Collins and a number of others, to meet him in Kansas City.

They decide to go to Dodge City in small groups and on 31 May, Earp, with four other men, stepped off the train at Dodge where they were met by 'Prairie Dog' Dave Morrow, who was wearing a special policeman's badge. Morrow agreed with Earp that Luke Short was being railroaded and agreed to help, and because it was illegal to wear guns in the city, appointed them special deputies. Bat Masterson and Charlie Bassett had already arrived, and with the sudden arrival of four more notorious gunfighters, the sheriff contacted the governor saying that gunmen were invading Dodge.

When Luke Short suddenly appeared off the train and it became known that Wyatt Earp and Bat Masterson were among the gunmen accompanying him, the local gunmen, led by a man called Webster, decided that discretion was the better part of valour and suddenly became less vociferous, muttering that maybe they should have talks to resolve the problem. A compromise was reached that allowed Luke Short to carry on his business, but the girls who worked in his saloons and gambling halls would have to be more discreet in their dealings with customers.

Wyatt Earp and Bat Masterson.

One year later, in 1884, Luke Short sold his business and went to Fort Worth, Texas, where he bought another saloon. He died in 1893 at the age of just 39 years old.

Wyatt Earp drifted around getting into a number of scrapes and was imprisoned a couple of time for minor offences. In 1902 he opened a saloon in Tonopah, Nevada, called the 'Northern Saloon', but despite his already growing reputation it failed and he moved on to various other ventures, including mining, all of which were unsuccessful. Wyatt Earp died in Los Angeles in 1929. A book written about his life, *Wyatt Earp, Frontier Marshall*, on which he had collaborated, was declared a 'pack of lies' by Virgil Earp's widow, Allie Earp.

The Northern Saloon, owned by Wyatt Earp, with two unknown young ladies in front.

An elderly Wyatt Earp in Hollywood standing beside a Packard car belonging to actor William S. Hart.

Josephine Marcus with Wyatt Earp at a mining camp in California.

Chapter 16

Bartholomew (Bat) Masterson

Bartholomew (Bat) Masterson was another feared gunfighter who became a Deputy US Marshal in 1876.

Born in Iberville County, Quebec, Canada, in 1853, the son of a prairie farmer, Masterson decided that the life of a farmer was not for him. With his two brothers, Ed and Jim, he headed for the United States.

His first encounter using a gun was in the town of Sweetwater, Texas, in 1876 while he was involved in a relationship with a local girl, Molly Brennan. An army sergeant by the name of Melvin King, from the local

Bat Masterson.

fort, also had an eye for the girl and when he found Bat Masterson and the girl enjoying a night out in the local saloon, he got drunk and pulled out a gun. He fired first, hitting Bat Masterson in the pelvis, but Masterson was more accurate and as he fell to the floor, he shot the sergeant dead. Masterson's injury caused him to carry a cane for the rest of his life.

After experiencing work as a buffalo hunter and army scout, during which he honed his skills as a gunfighter, Masterson became a lawman, joining his brother in Dodge City. His brother Ed Masterson was the marshal of Dodge City, Kansas, at the time and he invited his brother to join him. Bat Masterson's reputation as a gunfighter had been firmly established by this time and with another legendary lawman, Wyatt Earp, who was already a deputy city marshal in Dodge City, he made Dodge City one of the most law-abiding cities in the West.

Right: Ed Masterson.

Below: Dodge City Peace Commission. Top row, left to right: Will Harris, Luke Short, Bat Masterson, W.F. Petillon. Front row: Charlie Bassett, Wyatt Earp, Frank McLean, Neil Brown.

In 1877, at the age of 22, Masterson became sheriff of Ford County, while his brother Ed remained city marshal of Dodge. When Ed Masterson was gunned down and killed by a drunken cowboy by the name of Jack Wagner in 1878, his brother Bat, who was quickly on the scene, shot and killed the gunman. After being appointed marshal he put in place a 9pm curfew and a 'no gunplay' law, which he strictly enforced. Bat Masterson was voted out of office two years later after allegations in the local newspaper that he was taking bribes.

In 1879, the famous war between the two railroad giants, the Atchison, Topeka & Santa Fe and the Denver & Rio Grande broke out over the rights to build the railroad to Deadwood. Bat Masterson was appointed

The silver mining town of Creede, Colorado.

a Deputy US Marshal to help keep law and order. There were numerous shooting incidents between the two railroad crews, who often hired local gunfighters to assist them, but fortunately there were very few fatalities due in the main to the protection of the deputy US Marshals.

Over the next 10 years Bat Masterson became city marshal in the town of Creede and the town of Trinidad in Colorado. Coupled with his work in gambling halls and saloons, his reputation ensured a degree of peace in these towns and establishments.

His reputation as a gunfighter and stories of the number of men he had killed had followed him. Some elements were justified; others were embellishments of minor fracas. After being asked to leave Denver, Colorado, by the local sheriff because he refused to give up carrying his sidearm, Bat Masterson decided to move to New York City where he wouldn't have to defend his gun-fighting reputation.

For a short period he was involved in promoting boxing matches, but he then turned his interest in boxing and other sports into a new

Above: Saloon in Trinidad, Colorado.

Right: Bat Masterson in his later years.

career and joined the *New York Telegraph* as a sports writer. No doubt his reputation was a leading factor in his success. Although it was a profession far removed from his original one, he came to enjoy it. In 1905, President Teddy Roosevelt appointed Bat Masterson United States Marshal of the southern district of New York. He was dismissed in 1909 when William Howard Taft became President. Taft gave the reason that he had no use for a former gunfighter in his government's law and order programme, despite Masterson's hard work over four years.

Bat Masterson died on 25 October 1921 of a heart attack.

Chapter 17

Tom Smith

There was the odd law enforcement officer who never carried a gun yet was still able to maintain law and order wherever he went. One of these was Tom Smith.

Born in New York City in 1840, Tom Smith had from his childhood days wanted to be a policeman. Although not a big person, he was extremely able with his fists and had been taught the art of boxing. So proficient had he become, that he turned professional and for five years his 'purse' money fed the family. When he was 21 he joined the New

Tom Smith.

York Metropolitan Police Force and was assigned to the 18th Precinct. It was here that he came into conflict with a crooked gambler by the name of Ed Monahan, a man he was to encounter again some years later.

Tom Smith became one of the most respected members of the police force and gained himself a reputation for honesty and fairness. Then one night he chased a purse-snatcher up an alley and was about to shoot a warning shot over his head in an effort to make him stop, when he tripped over some rubbish as he fired. The bullet hit a 14-year old boy who was leaning over a balcony to see what was going on and killed him.

An enquiry exonerated Tom Smith, but the local people were outraged by the accidental shooting, claiming that the

Bear River, Wyoming.

department had swept the incident under the carpet. One month later Tom Smith resigned, unable to come to terms with the accidental death of the young boy, and headed west. He joined the 5th Infantry Regiment in Arizona and served with them for four years.

In 1868 Smith got a job driving the supply wagon for the Union Pacific Railroad and, during an evening's relaxation when he was seated at the poker table in a small town called Bear River, he accused the dealer of cheating. Despite being unarmed, Smith quickly dealt with the man using his fists. The owner of the gambling saloon, unknown to Tom Smith, was Ed Monahan. Monahan sent three of his men into the saloon to deal with Smith using their guns, but once again Smith's years of experience in the ring stood him in good stead and he quickly overwhelmed them.

The people of the small town were delighted and offered him the post of town marshal. Smith said that he would think about it, but that night Monahan, furious at having crossed swords with Smith for the second time and coming off worse once again, sent one of his hired gunmen after Tom Smith. Smith was streetwise – years of pounding the beat in New York City had seen to that – and he had been told that a man by the name of Montana Jones had been hired to take care of him.

He had realised that he was to become a target and had quickly come up behind the gunman and surprised him, knocking him to the ground. Carrying the limp body of the gunman over his shoulder, he strode into Monahan's saloon and dumped the body on the bar. He warned Monahan that the next time he would not be so gentle and would break more than a jaw.

Delighted with the way he had conducted himself, the town council pressed him once again to take up their offer. They had even borrowed a city marshal's badge from a nearby town, and this time Tom Smith accepted.

Several weeks passed before the name Monahan sprang up again. On this occasion Tom Smith had gathered information that Monahan was selling whisky to the Indians, and this was a federal offence. Accompanied by a troop of soldiers from Fort Bridger, Tom Smith went after Monahan. He had learned from the go-between that Monahan used in his dealings with the Indians, and who had been arrested by the military, that Monahan and eight of his men were planning to ambush Smith. That night Tom Smith burst in the back door of Monahan's place and placed him under arrest, while armed members of the town council took care of his men.

The go-between had no intention of taking the blame for the whisky peddling and implicated Ed Monahan. Monahan was tried by a military court and sentenced to ten years in the federal prison at Fort Leavenworth.

By this time the railway line that had slowly been making its way across the territory had moved on, and with it went the gamblers, gunmen and whores. The town settled down and the only trouble the town marshal had to deal with was the occasional drunk or rowdy cowboy on a weekend. This was too mundane for Tom Smith and he moved on to a rough little town in Colorado by the name of Greeley. He took up the post of town marshal and within a matter of months had cleaned the place up.

The railroad continued its way across America and in 1867 the Kansas-Pacific Railroad linked up with Chicago and Denver in Abilene. A man by the name of Joseph McCoy persuaded the citizens of Abilene to invest $150,000 to build stockyards so that when the massive Texas trail herds arrived they could be accommodated. As soon as they were built the gamblers, gunmen, outlaws and prostitutes turned up, eager to take money from the cowboys who would be bringing the cattle in. Prosperity for the town appeared to be just around the corner.

Abilene, Kansas, 1875.

When the first of the herds arrived in May 1867, it soon became obvious that the men who drove the cattle had not seen anything that resembled civilisation for months. The mayor of Abilene put up a notice saying that guns should not be worn in the town, but it was totally ignored and lawlessness threatened the once-sleepy settlement. No one wanted the job of town marshal, as the wearing of a badge seemed to make the wearer a target for drunken cowboys or, even worse, outlaws.

For three years the town suffered at the hands of the lawless crew that stayed in the town between trail herds, until one afternoon in June 1870 when Tom Smith rode into town. He went to the mayor's office and said, 'I understand you are looking for a marshal'.

Seeing that the young man before him was not wearing a gun, the mayor pointed out that a man without a gun in Abilene was signing his own death warrant. Tom Smith smiled and said that he would take the job and that the mayor should not worry about the fact that he was not wearing a gun.

The mayor, desperate for some law and order to be brought to the town, agreed and Tom Smith immediately gave him a sign to put up in town, which read:

June 4, 1870
Starting this date, carrying firearms is forbidden within the town of Abilene. Violators will be fined fifty dollars and will be ordered out of town.

Tom Smith, Town Marshal
Abilene, Kansas

Within hours the whole town knew of the new marshal and the fact that he never carried a gun. It was decided that they would welcome him in the traditional way, which was to tar and feather him and ride him out of town on a rail. They were then going to lynch him from the nearest tree. Tom Smith strode down the street towards the main saloon, where he knew the toughest of the gunmen would be. As he approached two of the gunmen stepped out onto the street and one of them had his pistols drawn. They were the 'welcoming committee'.

Smith politely informed them that guns were no longer allowed and advised them to hand them over. There was a shocked silence and then one of the men offered his gun to Tom Smith – barrel first. Smith half moved away, then struck and two gunmen suddenly lay sprawled on the dusty street. The marshal picked up the guns and strode over to the open-mouthed cowboys looking on and demanded their guns. The shocked men handed over their weapons without a murmur, realising that this was not a man to be trifled with. Within an hour every weapon was in the hands of the marshal and stored safely in his office, to be collected by their owners as they left town.

The next day a delighted mayor approached Tom Smith and congratulated him, but warned him that there were some who resented the fact that they couldn't wear their guns. One of these was Wyoming Frank, who told everyone that he would kill the marshal if he tried to take away his guns.

The mayor then asked Tom Smith if he knew a man by the name of Ed Monahan. Smith tensed immediately: this was the man he had had confrontations with in Bear River and New York City. Now he was running a crooked gambling saloon just outside Abilene.

That afternoon Wyoming Frank came swaggering down the street wearing his guns in open defiance. Tom Smith suddenly appeared in front of him and, before Wyoming Frank could draw his guns, he was knocked to the ground unconscious. Some of Wyoming Frank's friends moved toward the marshal, but a number of armed townspeople appeared to back him up. Frank's cronies were ordered to drop their guns and were taken to the local gaol, where each of them was fined 50 dollars and told to leave town.

Wyoming Frank was the last to be released and, as he was leaving, a shot rang out and he fell to the floor dead before he could tell Tom Smith who had paid him to try to kill the marshal. Smith dashed into the street to see a small shadowy figure on a horse racing away in the gathering gloom. Getting on the murderer's trail, he tracked him to a log cabin where he saw three men. One of them was a face from the past – Ed Monahan.

Realising he would need help, Smith raced back toward town, where he met a number of men riding towards him. Deputising them, he and the posse returned to the cabin. On arrival he found the body of the young man whom he recognised as the gunman he had been chasing, but there was no sign of Monahan and the other man.

The posse returned to town and rode immediately to Monahan's saloon. Confronting Monahan, Tom Smith ordered him out of the area of Abilene and, as an incentive to go, put a torch to the tent that held the saloon and all the gambling equipment. Monahan left the following day.

The town flourished as lawlessness decreased and a number of businesses sprang up, including saloons and gambling halls. Although the owners of the saloons and gambling establishments paid lip service to the town marshal by singing his praises loudly whenever the need arose, secretly they would have liked him out of the way. Among the new owners was Ben Thompson, a former city marshal and a feared gunfighter. He opened a gambling saloon and was quick to realise that without Tom Smith enforcing the law, his crooked gambling tables could make him a fortune.

One night he decided to kill the marshal and, as Tom Smith made his regular late-evening patrol of the main street, he fired two shots, but both missed. Tom Smith had realised some time before that the safest place to walk was either down the middle of the main street, or mingled with crowds that were still about. This gave any back-shooter or assassin a very limited target.

Smith's past came back to haunt him one evening when he arrested a young cowboy who was causing a disturbance while drunk and carrying a gun. He was arrested and hauled up before the local Justice of the Peace and fined 50 dollars. The young hothead refused to pay and was sentenced to 10 days in gaol. On hearing his sentence, the youth grabbed a gun from one of the deputies, ran into the street and jumped on the nearest horse. As he did so he fired at Tom Smith and missed, but his second shot hit the deputy in the leg. Smith grabbed a rifle and fired at the back of the lad as he raced away on the horse. The rider pitched forward and fell dead in the street.

The boy's father was incensed by the death of his son, and when he found out about Tom Smith's past experience in New York, when he had shot dead another young lad, he had the story published in the local newspaper. Although the local people agreed that the marshal had acted properly, it didn't take long for rumours to fly about. Tom Smith resigned as marshal and left Abilene.

Another attempt on his life later that month convinced Smith that Monahan was involved and that there was going to have to be a showdown between them. Word reached him that lawlessness had returned to Abilene, so he approached General Miles at Fort Leavenworth and asked to be appointed a Deputy US Marshal. In addition he asked that a troop of cavalry meet him outside Abilene, to help him rid the town of Monahan and the gunmen and outlaws under his control who now appeared to be running the town.

At the appointed time Tom Smith met with Major Gilford and his men and together they rode into Abilene. Within minutes the gunmen and outlaws, together with Monahan, were riding hell-for-leather out of town. The troopers gave chase and a number of outlaws were killed before the remainder of them gave themselves up, including Monahan. He was sent to Fort Leavenworth while the rest were kept in custody to come before the federal judge.

There were still factions within the territory who hated Tom Smith and the way he enforced law and order. Then, in November 1870, word came in that a man called Andrew McConnell had shot and killed his neighbour over a piece of disputed land. Tom Smith and deputy town marshal McDonald rode out to arrest McConnell. Later that day a rider raced into town saying that Tom Smith had been murdered. The witness said that he had seen Smith and McDonald ride up to McConnell's place and Tom Smith had gone inside, leaving McDonald outside. Then a man called Les Miles came out and pointed a gun at McDonald, who rode off leaving Smith alone. The witness then saw Smith come out with McConnell and Smith appeared to be wounded. He then saw Miles club Smith to the ground with his rifle and at that point the witness said he rode off to get help.

A large posse was quickly organised and rode out to the McConnell place. When the men reached it, they found the headless body of Tom Smith lying beside a chopping block, with the bloodstained axe lying nearby. The posse split up and started a search for McConnell and Miles and two days later they were found holed up in a cabin. After a brief struggle they were captured and taken to Fort Riley. It was feared that if they had been returned to Abilene they would have been lynched.

The two men were later sentenced to imprisonment for their part in the killing of Deputy US Marshal Tom Smith, but it could not be proved that they had actually killed him.

Chapter 18

Pat Garrett

Born on 5 June 1850 in Alabama, Patrick Floyd Garrett was the son of a wealthy plantation owner. However the Civil War wiped out the family's estate and fortune and like many other families in similar situations they found themselves almost destitute. Garrett's parents never recovered and died soon after General Lee had surrendered.

Pat Garrett then moved to Dallas County, Texas, where he obtained work as a cowhand for various ranches. In 1878 he joined up with a party of buffalo hunters and for the next three years earned his living as a professional buffalo hunter.

After losing the last of his money at the gambling tables in Tascosa, Garrett and two friends decided to head further west and see if they could make their fortune.

After a long hard ride that took several weeks, they approached Fort Sumner and found themselves desperately low on funds. Pat Garrett's two companions decided to move on further west, but Garrett made the decision to stay and find work. He approached a local rancher, Pete Maxwell, and found a job as a cowhand. After spending a year working on the ranch, during which time he married a local Mexican girl called Juanita Martinez, Pat Garrett got into a serious argument with Maxwell and was fired.

It was around this time that his wife died in childbirth and so Pat left to live in a village

Full-length portrait shot of Pat Garrett.

called Anton Chico. With money he had saved, Garrett opened a small restaurant in Fort Sumner and, after making a success of the business, was invited to go into partnership with the local merchant, Beaver Smith. All the time the town of Fort Sumner was expanding as more and more people moved west and settled in the area.

During this period Pat Garrett met and became very friendly with Henry McCarty, also known as William Bonney (Billy the Kid), and the two were often seen together drinking and gambling. Billy's reputation as a gunfighter was growing steadily and he had been seen associating with known rustlers. It was this that was to be the source of some concern with the local ranchers. With the local sheriff election coming up, John Chisum and a number of other powerful ranchers

Left: John Chisum, one of the most powerful ranchers in New Mexico.

Below: John Chisum's ranch in New Mexico.

THE OLD CHISUM RANCH BELOW ROSWELL, NEW MEXICO

put pressure on Sheriff Kimbrell to appoint Pat Garrett as his deputy. Behind the pressure was a plan to run Garrett against Kimbrell in the upcoming elections.

The local ranchers were increasingly concerned about the amount of rustling that was going on and were convinced that the presence of Billy the Kid in the town was attracting gunfighters and other outlaws who were out to enhance their reputations. Their thinking was that if Pat Garrett was elected sheriff he could stop Billy entering the territory because he was on friendly terms with him and knew all his ways.

Garrett was initially sceptical about accepting the position of deputy sheriff, when he heard the reasoning for his appointment. He had grown fond of Billy and felt that the Kid had been forced into a life of gunfighting and crime by circumstances beyond his control. But Garrett agreed to run for sheriff and when it became known that he was putting himself forward, Billy showed no resentment toward his friend, although he knew that the moment Pat Garrett was elected he would be asked to leave the territory. In fact Pat Garrett told Billy to his face that if he was elected he would ask him to leave the territory, and if he refused he would either arrest him or kill him.

Pat Garrett was duly elected sheriff and was also appointed a Deputy US Marshal, which gave him greater powers of arrest over a wider area. Pat Garrett made Billy his number-one priority and set about monitoring his movements.

Billy was soon in trouble again. Garrett had been warned about some counterfeit notes being used to buy cattle in Mexico and the owner of the notes was trying to find someone who would act for him. A man called Barney Mason, who was a member of Garrett's posse, agreed to act as buyer and left to meet up with him at an abandoned sawmill. As he left so did Billy the Kid, Dave Rudabaugh and Billy Wilson.

Pat Garrett organised his posse and headed toward the sawmill. As they approached Billy the Kid and his gang opened fire on them and left. The next morning the gang was

Pat Garrett, the sheriff who shot and killed Billy the Kid.

Dave Rudabaugh with two unknown friends.

cornered in the Greathouse and Kick Stage Station and surrounded by the posse. The gang was asked to surrender and a man called Jimmy Carlyle acted as spokesman for the posse and offered to act as an exchange hostage for Jim Greathouse, the owner of the stage station, while it was decided what to do. Carlyle went into the house and an hour later shots were heard and the body of Carlyle was hurled through a window. The body had three bullets in it and the other members of the posse claimed Billy the Kid had done it in an act of revenge.

That night Billy the Kid and his gang slipped away and a huge manhunt was mounted. Over the next few months cattle rustling became more prevalent and all indications were that the Billy the Kid and his gang were involved. Garrett then received word that a rancher by the name of Charlie Bowdre had been sheltering the Kid and his gang and wanted to meet with him. Garrett agreed on the condition that Bowdre came unarmed and they met at a quiet point. At the meeting Garrett pointed out to Bowdre that he was getting himself into trouble associating with Billy the Kid and his gang, and if he helped him capture the Kid, he would do what he could to protect him from prosecution.

Garrett also learned the next day that Frank Stewart, the local representative of the Canadian River Cattleman's Association of the Texas Panhandle, had arrived in Anton Chico. This was an organisation of the most powerful ranchers in Texas, who had got together to stamp out rustling and were prepared to go to great lengths to achieve that aim.

A meeting was arranged between Pat Garrett and Frank Stewart in Las Vegas, with the result that the Association placed a large number of men at Garrett's disposal, together with wagons full of supplies and ammunition. Their aim was to annihilate all the rustlers in Texas at any cost.

A trap was set in the old Fort Sumner, which was just outside the town, and word was got to Billy the Kid that Pat Garrett and Barney Mason were there hoping to catch him. Garrett ordered all the men now under his command to conceal themselves outside the fort, in the hope

Las Vegas in 1890.

that Billy would think that there were only two of them there. As the gang approached the fort, Billy, who up to this point had been in front, suddenly went to the rear of the group. Tom O'Folliard took his place and as they got within range, Garrett called for them to stop. The words were barely out of his mouth before the firing started. The gang turned their horses, but Tom O'Folliard was hit, having been mistaken for Billy. The gang escaped, leaving one of their men to die on the snow-covered ground of Fort Sumner.

The weather closed in and a heavy snowstorm blanketed the area, making it impossible to track the gang. Then word reached Garrett that the gang was at the Brazel ranch, so the posse re-formed and headed out. The snow had stopped, and finding no one at the Brazel ranch they pushed on. A few miles up the trail they came across some tracks leading to an old stone cabin near Stinking Springs with some horses behind. Surrounding the cabin they kept watch, then suddenly the door opened and Charlie Bowdre stepped out. A crackle of rifle fire caused him to stagger, then fall back into the shack.

One of the men inside the shack called to his horse and tried to get it to come in, but as it approached the door Garrett shot it dead, leaving the doorway blocked – the gang was trapped. Calling for the gang to surrender, the only reply he got was to come and get them!

The rock house at Stinking Springs in which Billy the Kid and his gang holed up before being arrested by Pat Garrett.

Above left: Charlie Bowdre, one of Billy the Kid's gang.

Above right: Pat Garrett (left) with James Brent and John Poe.

The following morning the gang surrendered, realising that they were in a no-win situation. The posse took Bowdre's body back to his home and distraught widow and then proceeded to Fort Sumner. The following day the prisoners were taken to Las Vegas where they would be put on a train to Santa Fé.

Word had reached the town that Sheriff Pat Garrett was bringing in Billy the Kid and his gang, and when Garrett arrived he was greeted by an armed mob surrounding the train. Garrett threatened the mob, which included Sheriff Desidero Romero and his deputies, that he would arm the gang if anyone attempted to interfere with their safe passage aboard the train and they could suffer the consequences.

Charlie Bowdre with his wife.

Billy the Kid offered to help Garrett if things got rough, knowing that Garrett wouldn't let anyone take his prisoners while he was alive. Garrett told Billy that it was not him they were after, but Rudabaugh, a member of his gang who had broken out of gaol in Las Vegas and killed one of the deputies.

One of the prominent citizens, who was also acting governor, stepped forward and placated the mob, saying that Garrett was only doing his job and that any interference by the citizens of the town could have severe consequences. The journey to Santa Fé was uneventful and Billy the Kid and his gang were handed over to the local sheriff to await their trial. Dave Rudabaugh remained in Las Vegas where he was tried for murder and for robbing the mails. He was convicted and sentenced to 20 years in prison, but later escaped to Mexico.

Dave Rudabaugh worked on a number of ranches while there, but was caught stealing cattle. He went to a little town by the name of Parral and took it over by instilling fear in the locals. His prowess with a gun was to be feared, but one evening he was involved in a card game when someone called him a cheater. He drew his gun and shot the man dead, then shot another dead who had also drawn his gun,

Dave Rudabaugh's head, mounted on a pole by the inhabitants of a small town called Parral, Chihuahua, Mexico.

and wounded another. Realising he was in trouble, he left, but could not find his horse and returned to the cantina. As he entered, gunshots rang out and he fell to the floor riddled with bullets. The locals then cut off his head, stuck it on a pole and paraded it through the streets.

In the meantime Billy the Kid was placed on trial for the murder of Sheriff Brady and after a short trial was convicted and sentenced to death, the sentence to be carried out in Lincoln County.

The journey to Lincoln was by train and took three days, Billy the Kid remaining shackled in handcuffs and leg irons the whole time. On reaching Lincoln, Billy the Kid was housed in an old storeroom because the gaol was crumbling and not fit to hold prisoners. Two guards, Bob Olinger and J.W. Bell, were assigned to watch Billy the Kid and Olinger made no secret about the fact that he detested the Kid.

While Olinger was on duty, no one was allowed to visit the Kid, but when Bell was on duty he would allow some visitors. One person who visited regularly was a man called Corbett who worked in a local store. On one visit he slipped a note to the Kid saying that there was a gun wrapped in newspaper at the bottom of the latrine pit.

Choosing a day when he knew Pat Garrett would be out of town carrying out his duties, Billy the Kid made his move. The guard Bell was lounging around when the Kid asked to use the latrines. Explaining that it was awkward using the latrine, he asked for the leg irons to be taken off. Bell told him that the only person with the keys was Pat Garrett. Billy the Kid entered the latrine and plunged his hand in, and found the bundle at the bottom. Despite the latrine having been searched every day, the guards never looked into the bottom of the latrine pit, which under the circumstances was understandable. As he left the latrine, the Kid pointed the gun at Bell and ordered him upstairs. Bell foolishly decided to make a run for it and ran downstairs. Billy fired and missed, but the ricochet hit the wall and hit Bell just below the armpit, killing him almost immediately. Hobbling back to

Above left: James Doolin and Bob Ollinger.

Above right: Bob Oliver who was shot dead by Billy The Kid during his escape from custody in Lincoln County.

the main room, Billy picked up Bell's shotgun. Crossing to the window he saw Bob Olinger, who had heard the shot, running across the street. Billy called out Olinger's name, which caused Bob Olinger to look up, and seconds later he was dead as Billy pulled both triggers on the shotgun.

Billy managed to beat the shackles off and, stealing a horse from outside the saloon, he rode out of town. It wasn't until the following day that Garrett learned of the escape and he set about tracking Billy. Following a number of leads, he heard that Billy was still in the area and visiting a girl at a house owned by a Pete Maxwell. Accompanied by two deputies Pat Garrett headed out towards the house in the middle of the night.

The two deputies took up a position on the porch while Garrett slipped in to Pete Maxwell's bedroom and gently woke him up. He warned Maxwell not to make a sound, and asked which room the Kid was in. The door suddenly opened and a youthful figure with a gun in his hand, but down at his side, stood in the doorway.

Deputy Sheriff Bob Ollinger.

'Quien es?' (Who's there?) came a soft voice. Without replying, Garrett immediately fired twice. The first bullet hit Billy the Kid in the heart, killing him instantly.

After the death of Billy the Kid, the people of Lincoln County seemed to resent Pat Garrett and the way he had killed Billy. With his term as sheriff at an end he did not seek re-election, recognising the fact that it was unlikely that he would get back in. He retired to his ranch near the Pecos River, but not everyone was upset with him and he was offered a captaincy in the Texas Rangers. For the next two years he continued to help keep law and order in the territory.

Garrett joined a detective agency that looked after the interests of the major cattle ranches in tracking down rustlers. He was extremely successful and the number of rustlers appearing in court increased dramatically, but suddenly, for no known reason, he quit and returned to his ranch.

It was to be five years before the name of Pat Garrett was to feature again, when he was appointed sheriff of Dona Ana County, New Mexico, to cover for Sheriff Numa Raymond who had been killed. It was an appointment that was to last for a further two terms of office.

It is accepted that Pat Garrett was not the gentle lawmen some thought he was, as a number of outlaws he arrested would have confirmed, but he was scrupulously fair and honest. At times he even went out of his way to help rehabilitate former outlaws, and one such was a man by the name of Billy Wilson.

Garrett had had dealings with Billy Wilson when he was sheriff of Lincoln County, and Wilson had carried out a mail robbery. He had never been caught. It was in his capacity as sheriff that he visited Uvalde, New Mexico, and it was during one of these visits that Billy Wilson's name came up.

Frightened that Pat Garrett might be looking for him, Billy Wilson sent one of his friends to talk to him. Garrett was genuinely surprised to hear that Billy Wilson was living in the area under an assumed name.

It was explained that Wilson was now married with a family, owned his own ranch and had become one of the most respected ranchers in the area. When asked what he intended to do about Wilson, Pat Garrett replied that he had no quarrel with Billy Wilson, and as far as the mail robbery incident was concerned, that was so many years ago that it was best forgotten.

Some months later Billy Wilson received a message from Pat Garrett, who had become sheriff of Dona Ana County once again, to call at his office to see him on urgent business. Full of trepidation, Billy Wilson went to see Pat Garrett, fully expecting to be arrested. Pat Garrett greeted him warmly and shook his hand. Trembling, Billy Wilson asked what Pat Garrett wanted to see him about. Garrett reached into a drawer and pulled out a letter and passed it over the desk. With trembling fingers Billy Wilson opened the letter and inside was a full pardon signed by President Grover Cleveland.

In 1901 Pat Garrett met President Theodore Roosevelt and struck up a friendship with him, and when Garrett's term as sheriff was up, Roosevelt appointed him collector of customs at El Paso.

After an incident at a 'Rough Riders' banquet, which President Roosevelt had invited Pat Garrett to attend, he fell out of favour. He was not reinstated when his term of office as collector of customs was up.

Pat Garret left El Paso and took up residence in Las Cruces, where he purchased several ranches that he rented out to cattlemen. One of these was a cattleman by the name of Wayne Brazel, who started keeping sheep and goats on the land. Garrett was a cattleman who had detested sheep, and he started talks with another cattleman, Carl Adamson, with regard to leasing the land to him.

While travelling in his buckboard to Las Cruces from his Bear Canyon Ranch with Carl Adamson, Garrett met up with Wayne Brazel and the two got into an argument over the leasing. Brazel maintained that Garrett became so incensed during the argument that he reached for a

Wayne Brazel (seated), a member of Pat Garrett's posse.

101

shotgun that was lying under the seat of his buckboard. Brazel then said that he drew his pistol and shot Garrett in self-defence. The first bullet hit Garrett in the heart, the second between the eyes.

Adamson had stepped down from the buckboard and was dealing with the horses when the shots were fired. Brazel tied his horse behind the buckboard, leaving the body of Pat Garrett lying on the trail, and sat beside Adamson. The two men went into Las Cruces to report the shooting to the sheriff. Wayne Brazel (seated) was arrested, but later bailed.

Captain Fred Fornoff of the New Mexico police carried out an investigation, and discovered a spent Winchester rifle cartridge behind a bush some distance away, together with tracks of a horse and footprints. A subsequent examination of the body showed that Pat Garrett had been shot in the back. Brazel was charged with the murder of Pat Garrett, but the jury accepted his version of the events and he was acquitted.

Friends of Pat Garrett always maintained that he had been killed by a paid killer in retribution for killing Billy the Kid. Whatever the truth, Pat Garrett was one of the most honest lawmen the West ever had.

Chapter 19

Bass Reeves

One of the most feared Deputy US Marshals in the lawless West in the late 1900s was Bass Reeves. Bass Reeves was born into slavery in Crawford County, Arkansas, in 1838, and took his surname from his owner, William Steele Reeves, who was the Arkansas state legislator at the time. When Reeves was eight the Reeves family, slaves and all, moved to Grayson County, Texas, where Bass served the son of Steele Reeves, George Reeves, who was the sheriff and legislator in Texas and later to become the Speaker of the Texas House of Representatives.

When the American Civil War erupted George Reeves joined the Confederate army with the rank of colonel of the 11th Cavalry Regiment, taking Bass with him. At some point during the conflict Bass Reeves gained his freedom. It is unclear how this came about, but one story is that Bass Reeves got into a fight with his 'owner' during a card game and so severely beat him that he had to flee. He fled to the Indian

Bass Reeves.

Territory where he lived among the Cherokee, Creeks and Seminoles, learning their languages and their customs, something that was to be of great use in later life. Life as a fugitive slave was tough because if he was caught he knew he would be killed for striking his owner and running away.

During the Civil War, while a fugitive, it is thought that Bass Reeves may have been with one of the guerrilla Union Indian bands in the territory, such as the Cherokee Pins. Or he might have served with the Union's First Indian Home Guard Regiment, composed mostly of Seminoles and Creeks, using an Indian name. The Five Civilized Tribes (Cherokee, Choctaw, Creek, Chickasaw and Seminole) fought on both sides during the conflict. Afterwards, the western portion of their territory was taken away from them and set aside as reservations for Plains Indian tribes (Comanche, Arapaho, Cheyenne, Apache and Kiowa), which had been subdued by the US military. Bass Reeves lived with the Indians until 1865 when slavery was abolished under the Thirteenth Amendment.

As a freedman, Bass Reeves left the Indian Territories and moved to Texas where he met a young lady by the name of Nellie Jennie. They married and moved to Van Buren, Arkansas, in around 1870 and for the next 10 years Bass Reeves was a farmer and fathered 11 children. In 1875 Judge Isaac Parker was appointed federal judge for the Indian Territories at Fort Smith, Arkansas, and in turn appointed James Fagan as US Marshal with instructions to appoint 200 Deputy US Marshals to police the territory.

It was around this time that Bass Reeves was struggling with the farm and looking to do something else. He had accompanied law officers as a scout and 'posseman' on a number of occasions when they were looking for fugitives in the Indian Territories. James Fagan had heard of Bass Reeves and the fact that he spoke several Indian languages, understood their customs and possessed excellent tracking skills seemed to make him the perfect choice for a Deputy US Marshal. Bass Reeves was approached by Fagan and offered the appointment; he immediately accepted and, it is said, became the first black deputy to serve west of the Mississippi River. There is some dispute over this, however, as in 1867 a posse was sent out from Van Buren after a stagecoach robbery had taken place and the driver, Fred Nicholls, was killed. It was said that a man known as 'Negro' Smith led the posse. Furthermore, the newspaper *The Cherokee Advocate* reported that on 14 September 1871, a Cherokee Indian by the name of Ross had killed a black Deputy US Marshal on the bank of the Arkansas River opposite

Fort Smith. The man was subsequently caught and brought up in front of a federal judge who sentenced him to be hanged for the murder of a federal officer.

Bass Reeves was given the assignment of Deputy US Marshal for the Western District of Arkansas, which also had the responsibility for the Indian Territories. This covered an area of 75,000 square miles, and although Judge Parker ordered that 200 Deputy US Marshals be appointed, in fact there were never more than 50 or 60 to cover this vast area. Research has shown that up to this time over 114 deputy marshals had been killed in the line of duty trying to maintain law and order. Even the Indian Police suffered at the hands of outlaws that roamed the Indian Territories, but not to the same extent. The majority of federal lawmen who died were within a 50-mile radius of the town of Muskagee,

Deputy US Marshal Bass Reeves.

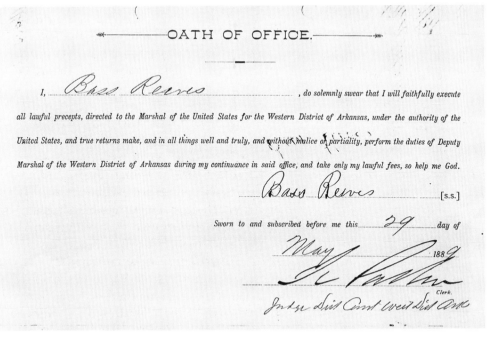

Bass Reeves's Oath of Office as a Deputy US Marshal, signed by Bass Reeves and Judge Isaac Parker.

Bass Reeves (sitting bottom left) with a number of Deputy US Marshals and town constables of the Muskagee Indian territory.

US Deputy Marshal Bass Reeves with a group of Deputy US Marshals.

Group of 12 lawman's badges.

which was regarded as being on the same lawless level as Dodge City, Tombstone and El Paso, Texas.

It was into this environment that Bass Reeves rode. He was an imposing figure on his large horse. He was 6ft 2in tall and weighed around 180lb. He was an expert shot with both rifle and pistol, equally good with both hands and an excellent horseman. As a Deputy US Marshal in the Indian Territories he had jurisdiction over white and black citizens who were not members of the tribes. Indian Police officers policed the Indian Territory, but any non-citizens who committed a crime against any Indian would have to be arrested by federal officers and their case heard in the federal court at Fort Smith. This meant that there had to be a considerable amount of cooperation between the Indian Police (Lighthorsemen) and the Deputy US Marshals, and that was where Bass Reeves came into his own, with his ability to speak several native languages.

Despite being sworn in as a Deputy US Marshal, Bass Reeves initially worked with a couple of experienced Deputy US Marshals, Robert J. Topping and Jacob T. Ayers. He acted as a posseman when they went into the Indian Territories. There was a federal rule that no Deputy US Marshal should travel alone into the Territories and should be accompanied by at least one posseman/scout. On the longer journeys

Above left: Badge of the Indian Police.

Above right: Indian police officer with his wife.

Indian Lighthorsemen.

a posseman/scout, a guard and a cook would accompany the deputy. They would use wagons to transport their supplies, which doubled up as prison wagons when they caught up with any fugitives. Every wagon was equipped with a long, heavy chain and at night the prisoners would be shackled together in pairs and the chain attached to the rear axle of the wagon. The other members of the deputy's party were not allowed to fraternise with the prisoners, for fear of the prisoners trying to get their weapons. There were often complaints from prisoners about being chained to the wagon for weeks and sometimes months before they got back to Fort Smith.

The Missouri, Kansas & Texas Railroad track that ran south through the territory was known as the 'deadline'. Deputies who crossed over the tracks took their lives into their own hands because, in the minds of many, the tracks marked the edge of civilization. Outlaws would leave their own 'wanted' posters on the trails warning certain Deputy US Marshals that they would be killed if they crossed the line. Over the years Bass Reeves featured on dozens of these posters. There were two main trails from Denison, Texas, that led to the Indian Territories and it was on these trails that horse-thieves and bootleggers could be found. The trails, known as the Seminole Trail and the Pottawatomie Trail, ran parallel with each other. Some deputies would not arrest anyone east of the tracks until they were on their way back to Fort Smith. The usual route for the lawmen to take was west to Fort Reno and Andarko, then south to Fort Sill and then back to Fort Smith. This was a journey of about 400 miles and could take up to two months depending on the weather.

Indian prisoners on the steps of Fort Smith courthouse.

Prison wagon known as a 'tumbleweed wagon', used by Deputy US Marshals when carrying prisoners on long trips across the state.

It was a dangerous business being a Deputy US Marshal, but the financial rewards could be very lucrative. The US Marshal was paid $90 per month, but the deputies were paid nothing and had to pay their own expenses, although the court paid the posseman $3 per day, the guard $3 per day and the cook $20 per month. The government allowed 70 cents per day to feed any prisoners they caught and six cents per mile for travelling, whether they were tracking a wanted criminal, delivering summonses, for which they were paid $2, or delivering court papers. For every prisoner they delivered to the court they were paid an additional $2. The trip to Fort Sill was estimated to take 30 days depending on the weather. Bass Reeves maintained that he never made a 30-day trip for less than $400. On one occasion he brought in 17 prisoners that he had arrested in various places in Comanche country and claimed a total $900 for fees. On occasions the Deputy US Marshals collected reward money that had been put up by the railroad companies or by the banks, if they caught a wanted fugitive.

The court in Fort Smith was the biggest and busiest in the territory and operated from 7.30am to 12 noon and 1pm to 6pm six days a week. Judge Isaac Parker's name became one of the most feared names in the West, because he handed out some of the most severe sentences. The court ran from 1875 to 1896 and during this period Judge Parker tried 13,490 criminal cases and secured 8,500 convictions. Sentences ranged from the death penalty in capital cases, to between one and 45 years in one of the state penitentiaries. In the case of death sentences being passed there was no appeal process: Parker's word was final. There was the odd exception when a Presidential pardon was granted, but during his time Judge Parker hanged 79 of the 88 he passed the death sentence upon. Of these 30 were white, 26 were Indians and 23 were black. Criminals knew that if they were arrested and taken before Judge Parker it was not just a question of sentence, but also the severity of the punishment he would hand out. Although Isaac Parker's record of executions dominated this period's history, he also worked to rehabilitate offenders, reform the criminal justice system, and advocate the rights of the Indian nations in the territory.

Over the years Bass Reeves adopted various methods of catching and arresting wanted criminals. One of these was to adopt various disguises, sometimes as a drifter, or a cowboy or even a preacher on one occasion. One arrest happened when he was given information regarding four wanted men who were holed up in a remote cabin. Dressed in farm overalls and driving a battered old buckboard, he deliberately managed to get the wheel of the buckboard jammed on a tree trunk. He went to the cabin to ask for help and when the four men obliged, he got the drop on them and made an arrest. Another time he feigned illiteracy and asked two wanted criminals if they would read something for him. As they studied the note Bass Reeves pulled out his handgun and promptly arrested them.

This photograph shows a group of robbers from Medicine Lodge, Kansas. The men in shackles are identified from left to right as: John Wesley, Henry Newton Brown, Billy Smith, and Ben Wheeler, the would-be robbers of the Medicine Valley Bank in Medicine Lodge, Kansas. Brown, a former member of Billy the Kid's gang, and Wheeler, a former outlaw and friend of Brown's, found themselves on the other side of the law with their appointments as deputy town marshals of Caldwell, Kansas. However, on 30 April 1884, Brown, Wheeler, Smith, and Wesley attempted to rob the Medicine Valley Bank. The robbery was unsuccessful and the robbers were eventually apprehended and brought back to Medicine Lodge, Kansas. Their time in gaol was brief as pandemonium erupted over their capture, creating a diversion for escape. In a hail of bullets, Henry Brown was shot dead while an injured Wheeler was captured and hanged beside Wesley and Smith.

Close-up of the manacled robbers John Wesley, Henry Newton Brown, Billy Smith, and Ben Wheeler.

In another incident Bass Reeves came close to losing his life when out looking for four men, two white and two black, on the Seminole whisky trail, who were all known to be 'bootleggers'. By chance he came across three brothers who were wanted for a string of crimes that included robbery, horse-stealing and a number of unsolved murders in the Indian Territory. The brothers, named Brunter, recognised Bass Reeves before he recognised them and immediately pulled their weapons. They ordered Bass Reeves to keep his hands away from his pistols and dismount from his horse. Bass Reeves showed the brothers the arrest warrants he was carrying in their name. He then asked for some information about where they had been and asked them politely if they were prepared to surrender themselves into his custody. The brothers found this very amusing considering they had their guns pointed at him, but relaxed long enough to allow Bass Reeves to whip out his six-guns and shoot dead two of the brothers and grab the gun of the third. As they struggled, Reeves managed to crack the outlaw over the head with his gun, unfortunately killing him. This of course meant that there would be no fees to be collected, as they only applied to those brought into court for trial.

The size of the posse that went after wanted criminals depended on whether or not they were considered so dangerous that more than one Deputy Marshal was required, or if it was a gang that had robbed a bank or a train. In addition to chasing after wanted men, Deputy US Marshals were also used as guards during executions. Bass Reeves's first guard duty at an execution was when a black man by the name of James Diggs was executed for the murder of a cattle drover in the Indian Territories. Hanged at the same time was an Indian called Postoak, who was convicted of murdering a white man, John Ingley, and his wife at their home in the Creek Nation. The fact that both these men had committed a crime against a non-citizen of the Indian Nation made it a federal court's business to pursue, and in both these cases, convict. If an Indian committed a serious crime against another Indian while in the Indian Nation, it fell to the elder of the tribe to sentence the person. In the event of it being a capital offence that carried the death penalty, in the formative years they carried out the sentence themselves. The Choctaw Indians had their own method, as can be seen in the photograph. This practice was later stopped and all executions were carried out by the US Marshal or sheriffs, depending in which state the offence took place.

Transporting prisoners who had been sentenced to varying terms of imprisonment in various penitentiaries was another role for the Deputy US Marshals. On one occasion Bass Reeves, together with

Choctaw execution of Silan Lewis, the last to be carried out by the tribe itself.

Choctaw Nation Light Horsemen about to go on patrol.

US Marshal's 'Paddy Wagon' used for transporting prisoners throughout the territories.

Deputy US Marshals Jacob Ayers, Thomas Lacy, J.M. Caldwell, Addison Beck and George Maledon, escorted 21 prisoners from Fort Smith to the House of Correction in Detroit, Michigan. Deputy US Marshal George Malendon was the official hangman at Fort Smith. Among the prisoners was one female by the name of Arena Howe, who had been sentenced to 10 years' imprisonment. There is no record of the offence for which she was sentenced, but it must have been a very serious one for her to receive a 10-year sentence. Her two children accompanied her, one aged six, the other an infant who had been born in the gaol at Fort Smith. There was no provision for the children of convicted felons, and as there was obviously no family to help, it was left to the prison authorities to do what they could. One has to assume that they served the sentence with their mother.

Arresting bootleggers who were selling rotgut whisky to the Indians was a regular thing and those caught usually faced a term of imprisonment of between 18 months and two years, plus a fine. The word 'bootlegger' comes from the use of a flat bottle that could easily be slipped down the side of a boot, thus making it easier to transport liquor into the 'dry' Indian Territories. The Oklahoma towns differed from the towns in the Indian Territories inasmuch as all the saloons in Oklahoma could legally sell liquor. The border towns were hot spots for the buying of liquor, which was transported into Indian Territory to illegally sell at an extortionate profit. It was the whisky trails, as they were known, that were frequented by both bootleggers and lawmen alike. Because the federal court for Oklahoma was in Guthrie, nearly all

Silver Spur Saloon.

Deputy US Marshals were cross-deputised so that they could operate freely in both territories.

One of these saloons, 'The Corner', which was on the border of the Seminole and Chickasaw nations, had a reputation for being the main distribution centre for illegal liquor. This was literally the 'Last Chance Saloon', because it was the last place to get an alcoholic drink before crossing the border into the Indian Territories. Bass Reeves was a frequent visitor to the saloon in the hope of catching bootleggers in the act of carrying illegal alcohol over the border. It is said that on a couple of occasions he was involved in personal gunfights after being challenged by bootleggers.

Bass Reeves wasn't perfect as a lawman and on 8 April 1884, while on a mission into the Chickasaw Nation, he shot and killed his black cook, William Leech. The posse was camped on the banks of the Canadian River when Reeves made comments about Leech's cooking. The other possemen assumed that it was part of the general banter that was usual between the two of them, as Leech had been the cook on a number of Bass Reeves's posses. One witness claimed that the banter became heated and that Leech grabbed hold of a puppy belonging to Bass Reeves and poured hot fat down its throat. The witness then said that Reeves whipped out his handgun and shot Leech dead. For some unknown reason, or maybe because of Reeves's reputation, nothing was ever done about it.

The following year Reeves was involved with the swearing-out of a warrant for the infamous female outlaw Belle Starr and her companion Fayette Barnett, for horse stealing. Having dealt with Belle Starr before on a number of occasions, Bass Reeves knew her well enough to suggest to her that she hand herself in to the court at Fort Smith. Belle Starr did just that, stating that she had no intention of letting herself be dragged into court by a federal Deputy US Marshal.

Out of the blue, a warrant was issued for Bass Reeves' arrest on the charge of the first-degree murder of William Leech. For the next six months he was held in the gaol at Fort Smith before his trial in October 1887. In order to pay for his attorney, Bass Reeves had to sell his home and use all his savings. At his trial he stated that he had shot William Leech, but it was an accident. He explained that a bullet had jammed in his Winchester rifle and he was trying to extract it with a knife when it went off. The bullet hit Leech in the neck and, despite sending for a doctor, Leech died before he arrived. Bass Reeves was acquitted of the charge and resumed his duties as a Deputy US Marshal. One school of thought was that the charge against Bass

Reeves was racially and politically motivated, but there is no evidence to support this.

The attempted bribing of Deputy US Marshals was not uncommon and no doubt there was the odd occasion when, for a relatively minor offence, it happened. Bass Reeves remembered one incident when he was riding as posseman for Deputy US Marshal Jacob Ayers, when they arrested a man called Bill Wilson for an assault and attempt to kill another man in the Choctaw Nation. Taking their prisoner with them, the posse went into Texas to arrest another white man for larceny in the Indian Territory. The man, William Watson, was duly arrested, and during the trip back to Fort Smith he asked if they could stop by the house of a friend of his, King Williams. The reason he gave was to obtain some money from his friend. Williams came out of his house and Watson asked to borrow some money. Williams offered him $100. Watson then asked to speak to Jacob Ayers privately and asked how he much wanted to let him go. Jacob Ayers promptly informed him that he was now going to be charged with attempting to bribe a federal officer. Over the next few days, as the posse and prisoners rode back, Watson again tried to bribe Ayers, only this time through Bass Reeves. Reeves told Watson he would have to talk to Ayers not him, but told him that there was no way Ayers could be bribed. It transpired that the charges of attempting to bribe a Deputy US Marshal were later dropped.

Not all the criminals were hardened outlaws. Bass Reeves was involved, together with Jacob Ayers, in arresting two peace officers, one white and one Indian: James Jones, Chief of the Indian Police of the Wichita Indian agency at Anadarko, and Indian Police Officer John Mullins, also known as Comanche Jack. They were charged with the murder of two white men, Charley Hard and James Davis. James Jones had arrived in the timber camp with some of his Indian Police with a warrant to arrest Hard, as he was wanted in Texas. Davis, however, worked in the timber yard and was not known to be wanted by anyone. His only connection with Hard was that Hard lived with Davis and his family, but because of the close association Davis was accused of being an accomplice. Jones told Davis that he was not under arrest, but he would have to accompany them back to Fort Sill for questioning. In the meantime Deputy US Marshal Ayers, together with Bass Reeves, had arrived at the Indian Police encampment at the Wichita Agency, Anadarko, and was told that Charley Hard and James Davis had been taken and were being held at Fort Sill.

Ayers immediately sent a telegram to Jones at Fort Sill saying that he wanted James Davis placed under arrest and brought back to him. No specific charges had been laid against Davis at this point, and no mention had been made of Charley Hard. Jones said that as he was making arrangements to transfer Davis, three men arrived identifying themselves as deputy sheriffs from Henrietta, Texas, and said that they wanted to take both Hard and Davis back to Texas to face criminal charges. After satisfying himself that the three men were lawmen, Jones released the two men into their custody. That was the last time they were seen alive.

James Jones met with Deputy US Marshal Ayers and explained the position and told him that he was concerned for the two men's welfare as he thought they could be lynched if they were returned to Texas. But Ayers wasn't satisfied and ordered Jones to surrender his weapon. Bass Reeves took the weapon and noticed that there were only four bullets instead of the usual six. It was not unusual to have five bullets in a pistol, as the hammer would rest on an empty chamber to prevent an accidental firing, but four was unusual for an experienced lawman. Removing the remaining bullets, he returned the weapon to Jones, noting that the bullets he had removed were copper-cased .45 Long Colt cartridges. After further investigation by Ayers and Reeves a number of witnesses said that they saw three men riding north towards where Jones had said he had handed the two men over to the Texas lawmen. Other witnesses said that they later saw five men riding south, and one was definitely identified as James Davis, as he was personally known to one of the witnesses. One month later Comanche Jack arrived at Fort Sill and told the army adjutant that he had discovered two bodies in a deep gulch. The army investigated and discovered that both men had been hanged then shot. They also found a copper-cased .45 Long Colt spent cartridge.

At a hearing, James Jones was asked about the circumstances regarding the handing over the two men to the Texas lawmen. Jones said that the deputy sheriffs of Henrietta had arrived with a writ for both men so he handed them over. When asked for the name of the sheriff at Henrietta whose name was on the writ, Jones said he had forgotten it and hadn't bothered to write it down in his notes. When asked about the cartridge found at the scene of the crime, a type used only by the army and the Indian Police, Jones could not give an explanation. After a lengthy trial both James Jones and Comanche Jack were found not guilty due to insufficient evidence. The three deputy sheriffs from Texas were never traced, and the mystery of who had lynched and shot Charley Hard and James Davis was never solved.

Bass Reeves continued to uphold the law throughout the Indian Territories and in 1884, together with Deputy US Marshal Charles LeFlore, he arrested one of the most notorious Texas horse-thieves, Robert Landers, in Fort Smith itself. The same year Reeves was involved in a gunfight that was to make headlines in the *Muskagee Indian Journal* newspaper. The largest ranch in the Chickasaw Nation was the Washington-McLish Ranch, the foreman of which was a man by the name of Jim Webb. Webb had a fearsome reputation for violence and had reportedly been responsible for the deaths of 11 men while ranching in the Brazos River region of Texas. Reeves became involved with Webb when Webb shot dead a black preacher who had let a fire on his farm (which was adjacent to the Washington-McLish Ranch), get out of control and spread onto the neighbouring land, causing considerable damage. Not satisfied with verbally berating the preacher, the hot-tempered Webb had killed him. Bass Reeves was sent to arrest Webb, which he did without any problem, but within days Webb had escaped and Bass Reeves was forced to go on a manhunt.

After some weeks Bass Reeves discovered Jim Webb in the process of buying provisions at the Bywaters Store at the foot of the Arbuckle Mountains. Bass Reeves made himself known to Webb and asked him to surrender. Webb refused and opened fire on Bass Reeves and a gunfight ensued. After some minutes Webb managed to get to some rocks at the foot of the mountains in an attempt to make his getaway. Bass Reeves calmly removed his rifle from its scabbard on his saddle and from a distance of about 400 yards put two bullets into Jim Webb, killing him. The storeowner witnessed the whole episode, together with a number of cowboys who were in the store at the time. This feat only served to enhance Bass Reeves's reputation, and a number of newspaper articles were written about the fearless, sharp-shooting, black Deputy US Marshal who maintained law and order throughout the Indian Territories.

Reeves escaped many assassination attempts during his career, one of the last occurring on the evening of 14 November 1906, at Wybark, Creek Nation. While riding in his buggy looking to serve warrants, unknown parties fired on him from under a railroad trestle. He returned fire, but nobody was hit. The would-be assassins were never found and Reeves continued to focus on arresting black and Indian felons, though he would still arrest white outlaws if the occasion called for it.

The last major gunfight that Reeves took part in erupted in Muskogee on 26 March 1907. A large group of black anarchists calling themselves the United Socialist Club had taken over a two-storey house and declared that they could claim any property in town. Two city constables, John Colfield and Guy Fisher, were sent with eviction papers, only to be met at the door of the house by gunfire. Fisher was wounded, but escaped; Colfield was severely wounded and couldn't move from where he lay. The US Marshal's office was alerted, and Chief Deputy US Marshal Bud Ledbetter, along with a black Deputy US Marshal named Paul Smith and others, arrived on the scene. An intense gunfight followed. Ledbetter killed two of the offenders, and Smith saved Ledbetter's life by killing one of the radicals who had Ledbetter pinned down. Reeves arrived late. After noting where most of the gunfire was coming from, he shot an anarchist who was shooting down on the lawmen from an upstairs window. The lawmen killed two more of the group before the remaining seven anarchists surrendered. Constables Colfield and Fisher recovered from their wounds, and Ledbetter called Reeves 'one of the bravest men this country has ever known'.

Even before that shootout, on 8 March 1907, the Oklahoma City *Weekly Times-Journal* ran a story headlined 'He has Killed Fourteen Men: A Fearless Negro Deputy of the Indian Territory'. Two days later, on 10 March, *The Washington Post* reprinted that lengthy article. It would be the most national exposure Bass Reeves received during his lifetime. And if accurate, the black anarchist he killed later that month would have been number 15.

When Oklahoma became a state on 16 November 1907, the federal office was downsized and many of the lawmen found other jobs. Bass

Close-up shot of four Deputy US Marshals attached to Fort Smith. Bass Reeves is on the far left.

Head and shoulder shot of Sheriff Bud Ledbetter.

Reeves, now 68, took a job with the Muskogee police department, walking a downtown beat. Old-timers reported that Reeves would walk with a sidekick who carried a satchel full of pistols and that there was never a crime on his beat. Reeves completed 32 years of service as a law officer without ever being reported wounded. He died at home of Bright's disease on 12 January 1910, aged 71, and was buried somewhere in Muskogee. The exact location is not known today; it was probably either in the Old Agency cemetery or in a small black cemetery west of town on Fern Mountain Road. Reeves's long service and remarkable dedication to duty could match any lawman of his time, and his six-shooter had been, as the two newspapers reported in March 1907, 'a potent element in bringing two territories out of the reign of the outlaw, the horse thief and bootlegger, to a great common wealth'.

Over his 32-year career as a Deputy US Marshal, Bass Reeves arrested 3,000 felons, killed 15 men and was never shot himself. His reputation for persistence, his total fearlessness, his skill with a gun and his ability to outsmart outlaws struck terror into lawbreakers. Deputy United States Marshal Bass Reeves was the real badass lawman of the Old Wild West.

Chapter 20

Grant Johnson

Grant Johnson was born into slavery in April 1854 in northern Texas; the exact location is not known. His father, Alex Johnson, who was a Chickasaw Indian slave and his mother, Miley Johnson, a Creek Indian slave, probably took the name Johnson from their owner. Grant Johnson grew up speaking fluent Muskogee, the language of the Creeks and Seminoles, and evidently received a good education as his signatures on court documents attest.

Although Johnson was noted as being African American, he also had strong American Indian features. He was what some referred to as a 'black Indian' or a 'mixed blood'. He was in fact a Creek freedman. Indian freedmen were either former black slaves of Indians, or descendants of Indian slaves of the Five Civilized Tribes (Cherokee, Choctaw, Chickasaw, Creek and Seminole). Grant Johnson has been in danger of being overlooked by historians, mainly because of another black lawman, Bass Reeves, who became better known to Western historians and the general public.

Johnson and other freedmen worked as lawmen in Indian Territory, as tribal policemen or Deputy US Marshals. Johnson clearly rates as one of the most important black lawmen in the history of Indian Territory. Some even felt he was better than Bass Reeves, but this comes down to a matter of opinion not deeds, because both were exceptionally good at their professions.

Deputy US Marshal Grant Johnson.

Indian police officers.

Grant Johnson became a Deputy US Marshal in 1888. He was about 5ft 8in tall, considerably shorter than his friend Bass Reeves at 6ft 2in, and weighed around 160lb. He wore a large, wide-brimmed white hat and a black bandana around his neck. He carried two revolvers on his hips and kept a Winchester rifle in a saddle scabbard on his horse, usually a black or a bay. Grant Johnson was a tough man in a tough land, but he exuded a quiet confidence to almost everyone he met. Such was his growing reputation, that newspapers not only in Indian Territory and Arkansas, but also in Kansas, Texas and the Midwest, covered his exploits. The following story appeared in *The Dallas Morning News* of 5 March 1891:

Map of Oklahoma showing the different tribal territories.

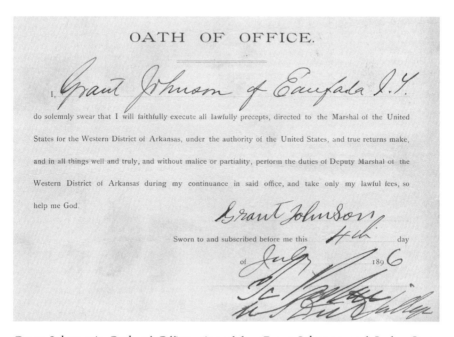

Grant Johnson's Oath of Office, signed by Grant Johnson and Judge Isaac Parker.

SHOOTING ON A TRAIN
A United States Marshal and a Supposed Escaped Convict Exchange Shots.

DENISON, Tex., March 4 1891
Quite an exciting shooting scrape occurred last night on Missouri, Kansas &
Texas passenger train No. 3, southbound, near Checotah, I.T. From one of the
trainmen The News correspondent gathered the following:

> *When the train stopped at Checotah, a rough-looking man with a broad, white*
> *hat passed into the second-class coach and took a seat near the stove. United*
> *States Deputy Marshal Grant Johnson, who got on the train at Muskogee,*
> *thought he identified the man as one he arrested several months ago on a*
> *charge of murder and had made his escape while in route to Fort Smith, so,*
> *passing down the aisle by the side of the new passenger, he stopped at the*
> *door and then passed into the next coach. He was then convinced that the*
> *new passenger was the man wanted. Johnson examined his pistol and opened*
> *the door to return to the second-class coach but was met on the platform by*
> *the stranger, who immediately opened fire. The marshal drew his pistol and*
> *returned the salute. The train was making…about 30 miles an hour, and the*
> *balls from the desperado's pistol flew wide of their mark and were buried in*
> *the end of the first-class passenger coach. During the shooting the escaped*
> *murderer jumped from the train, and whether or not he was wounded is not*
> *known. In all eight shots were fired. Quite a panic prevailed throughout the*
> *train as it was supposed it had been attacked by robbers.*

An article in the *Indian Journal* of Eufaula in the Creek Nation in
1901 said Johnson had held a Deputy US Marshal's commission for
14 years, which meant that he would have entered federal service in
1888. He probably worked as a posseman for other deputy marshals
for a number of years before being considered for the post of Deputy
US Marshal, because his name doesn't show up in the newspapers, or
bringing criminals to Fort Smith, Arkansas, the court of Judge Isaac C.
Parker, until 1890. He was described by Judge Isaac Parker 'as one of
the best deputy marshals he had worked with or known in the Indian
Territories'.

Grant Johnson had a home in Eufaula, Alabama. Before the Civil
War the most important Creek settlement in the area was at North
Fork Town. After the war the Missouri, Kansas & Texas Railroad built
a line through Indian Territory, and most of North Fork Town's citizens
moved three miles west to Eufaula, which was on the line. Some of the

Eufaula residents who were interviewed in the 1930s said Deputy US Marshal Johnson was the only law officer in the area during the town's formative years. James M. Calhoun said, 'Grant Johnson, a mulatto, of Eufaula, was the best Marshal they ever had'.

One of the roles of the Deputy US Marshal was to maintain law and order whenever and wherever required. One example of this was at Eufaula's Emancipation Day celebrations. Maintaining some semblance of order without spoiling the celebrations required the same quick-thinking that Grant Johnson used to get his man and stay alive in Indian Territory. The Indian freedmen always held two picnics, one at each end of town, and Grant Johnson could not possibly be in both places at the same time to keep the peace. However, he did own two distinctive-looking horses, a black one and a white one. Early on the morning of the celebration picnic, he tied one horse to a tree in full view of the crowd at one end of the town's main street. Then, when the festivities began later in the day, he rode the other to the other end of town, tied it to a hitching rail and mingled with the crowd. The people who saw his horse back at the opposite end assumed he was somewhere in the crowd and watching everything and everybody. It turned out to be one of the quietest Emancipation Day celebrations Eufaula ever witnessed.

In an interview with one of the early settlers, Nancy E. Pruitt, she was asked why she thought the federal government had decided to hire dark-skinned men to uphold the law in the area. 'Bass Reeves and Grant Johnson were coloured officers,' she said. 'They could talk Creek, and the Creeks liked Negroes better than they did whites is probably the main reason they had coloured officers'. The one thing that was said about both men was that never used devious means for arrest.

On 24 September 1892, a white woman named Mattie Bittle wrote Bass Reeves a letter, rife with misspellings, complaining about her husband:

Mr. Bass Reeves sir
I though I would write a few lines to you. I never never can get to see you. I want you to come soon as you can get here. My husband on the first Sunday in August beat me all most to death. I was real sick I wanted him to go for a doctor he said I need no doctor I was able to work as he was I said I wished he had stade in the penitintry he got a stick and beat me I don't think I can get over it they hindred him as he would killed me he is in Redfork I gess.

Mrs. Matie Bittle

Deputy US Marshal Reeves was not able to investigate the case, so he asked his friend and colleague Grant Johnson to deal with it for him. On 9 October Grant Johnson requested a warrant for George Bittle on a charge of assault and battery with intent to kill. In the request Johnson stated that Mrs Bittle was in bed at William Arnold's house and was not expected to live. The request was denied, with no reason given. After Mattie Bittle died, Johnson repeated his request to officials at Fort Smith. This time he got his warrant, and he arrested George Bittle on 16 October 1892 at Red Fork in the Creek Nation. The outcome of the case is not known, as it does not appear in the federal criminal file.

The following year Grant Johnson dealt with rustlers, as reported in *The Dallas Morning News* of 6 January 1893:

CATTLE STEALING MYSTERY CLEARED

KANSAS CITY, Jan. 5 — Two arrests made here are expected to clear up the mystery of huge cattle thefts in the Creek nation. W.H. Heath and his son, G.W. Heath, were arrested on a warrant charging them with stealing 31 head of cattle from the range near Checotah and shipping them here. Last night Deputy United States Marshal Grant Johnson of Eufaula, I.T., arrived with a United States warrant sworn out by T.W. Turk, a well-known ranchman, and says eight other arrests are to follow. Turk says the Heaths have been at the head of a gang which are engaged in running cattle off the ranges.

Three months later, on 17 April 1893, *The Emporia Daily Gazette* in Kansas discussed Johnson's police work:

CRIMES IN THE TERRITORY
Meat Thieves Captured
EUFAULA, Ind. Ter., April 17 — For the past six weeks the meat thief has been living high in Eufaula. During this length of time he has made away with about 500 pounds in all, and it seemed almost impossible to catch him. Last night he got into Marion Horn's smokehouse and relieved him of about 200 pounds and departed without even leaving his card. Mr. Horn reported his loss to Deputy Marshal Grant Johnson, and he immediately went in search of him. Late evening he came in with Bill and Ned Yates, brothers, charged with the offense. He has strong evidence against them and will at once take them to Fort Smith.

In July 1893 Grant Johnson, together with Bass Reeves, made an important arrest. Back in October 1890 in Harrison, Arkansas, Abner

Brasfield, a white man, killed Justice of the Peace William Ham and was later convicted of the crime. While his case was under appeal, Brasfield escaped into Indian Territory, where three years later Johnson, Reeves and posseman Andy Deering arrested him at a dance in Brooken, Creek Nation. But the next day, while Johnson and Reeves were at breakfast, Brasfield, with the help of family members, got away from Deering.

The Dallas Morning News reported on 22 July 1893:

SHOT HIMSELF FREE

EUFAULA, I.T., July 21—At 8 o'clock quite a flurry of excitement was caused by rapid shots in the eastern part of town. The cause was soon found to be the escape of Abner Brasfield [sic]. He escaped from the authorities and officers of Arkansas after having been convicted and sentenced to 21 years imprisonment for murder. The officers arrested him night before last at Brooken, surprising him completely. Deputy Grant Johnson caught him around the arms and waist and carried him from the building. His friends followed to Eufaula, and his father, it is alleged, gave him a pistol. His father was immediately placed in irons and A.B. Brasfield was also arrested, charged with aiding the escape. Some 10 or 12 shots were fired, but no one was hurt.

Abner Brasfield eventually turned himself in and, after doing time in prison, returned to Eufaula and served as an assistant to Grant Johnson. This is a perfect example of men who had been in trouble with the law and had served time in prison, being used as lawmen mainly because they knew other outlaws and where they were likely to hide out. It would also hopefully give them a chance to lead a reformed, crime-free life. It is an accepted fact that many lawmen in the West around this time had criminal records.

Another interesting case came in 1895, involving another white man, Wade Chamberlee, who had been originally arrested for harbouring outlaws involved in a train robbery at Blackstone Switch. Chamberlee had been arraigned at the federal court in Muskogee, but was released after a preliminary hearing, there being insufficient evidence to hold him. On hearing new evidence, a grand jury indicted him on 11 February 1895 and issued a warrant for his arrest. The next day Chamberlee rode into town and spoke with Grant Johnson; neither man was aware of the indictment. Later Deputy US Marshal George Lawson sought out Chamberlee to re-arrest him, and asked Johnson if he knew the man well enough to point him out. Having met with Chamberlee only a few hours earlier, Grant Johnson laughed and said he might be able to, then the two deputies arrested Chamberlee while he was in one of Muskogee's 'finest' establishments.

Up to this point, Grant Johnson had always brought in his felons alive, but on a fateful day in June he killed his first man in the line of duty. 'Deputy Marshal Grant Johnson killed a whisky peddler near Eufaula on Monday,' reported the *Fort Smith Elevator* on 7 June 1895. 'He ran on to three of them when they made fight, killing one and capturing the other two'. (It is uncertain whether the outlaw Johnson had shot in 1891 on the Missouri, Kansas & Texas train had died or not).

Then in July, according to *The Kansas City Times*, Johnson went to the famous criminal hiding place known as 'Younger Bend' in the Cherokee Nation and captured a man named John Moore, who was charged with assaulting his wife. Younger Bend had gained notoriety through an earlier resident – Belle Starr, 'Queen of the Oklahoma Outlaws' – who had used the place during her cattle-rustling escapades. Also in July, Johnson arrested Israel Carr, a young Creek who more than a year earlier had killed a white man, William Conway, near Okmulgee in the Indian Territories. That October, Johnson brought into custody a man named Jonah Bristow, who lived near Eufaula and had whipped his own son to death.

In 1889–90 the United States established federal courts in Indian Territory at Muskogee, Ardmore and McAlester with limited jurisdiction, while Fort Smith in adjacent Arkansas held on to capital cases. By 1896 the Fort Smith court no longer had jurisdiction in Indian Territory, and the three new courts assumed those federal powers. Judge Parker died that year, and the government transferred many of his former deputies to the new Indian Territory courts. The *Muskogee Phoenix* reported in September 1896 that 'A petition has been circulated in Eufaula and sent to Marshal Rutherford requesting that Grant Johnson be made an officer of the Muskogee court with headquarters at Eufaula'. Indeed, the transfer happened soon after, and Grant Johnson was headquartered at Eufaula for the duration of his federal service. He worked under US Marshal Rutherford and later US Marshal Leo Bennett, both headquartered at Muskogee.

Johnson's duties included trying to maintain order at the traditional Indian ball games, which were popular but not always peaceful pastimes in the Creek Nation. On 7 September 1899, the *Muskogee Phoenix* ran this report from the *Checotah Enquirer*:

The big Indian ball game that was advertised to come off last Wednesday between the Eufaula and Okmulgee 'towns' resulted in a free-for-all fight between the two teams, and the game was declared off. When the ball was first tossed up, the scrapping began and continued for two or three minutes, when Deputy Marshal Grant Johnson, of Eufaula, got among them and caused them to scatter by shooting in the ground.

On 11 June 1900, according to the next day's *Dallas Morning News*, Johnson brought in from Proctor, west of Eufaula, a young Creek charged with murdering his fiancée earlier that month. That fall the *Muskogee Phoenix* reported that Johnson brought three men to Muskogee to be tried for 'attempt at train wrecking' on the Missouri, Kansas & Texas line.

One of the best-known gunfights in which Grant Johnson participated took place on Christmas Day 1900 in Eufaula. In a 1938 interview one of the early residents, J.S. 'Shorty' Brown, who witnessed the incident (but gave the wrong date), said:

John Tiger, a Creek Indian, came to town one day in 1899. He was very drunk, and his wife had to drive the team part of the way. Upon reaching Eufaula, John stopped in front of a small restaurant. He had two guns, a Winchester, the other a six-shooter, and being too drunk to know what he was doing, he picked up his guns and began firing at the people on the street. Before the 'law' could stop him, he had killed three men, and there was a small boy some distance from him who had some of his waist buttons shot from his pants. Tiger saw the United States Marshal, Grant Johnson, who was a Negro, coming and knew that his game was up, so he ran for a short distance, and then stumbled over a low fence. He then started firing with his six-shooter at the marshal. There were two large trees between John Tiger and Grant Johnson, and each one took to a tree for protection. While fighting, the bullets could be heard hitting the trees. The marshal shot Tiger in the arm and captured him. The people in Eufaula were in a panic and wanted to string John Tiger up, but Mr. Foley quieted the mob and prevented them from lynching John Tiger.

Eufaula's citizens applauded Grant Johnson for his swift action and *The Indian Journal* reported on 25 January 1901 that:

The people of Eufaula made a purse a few days since and sent it to Grant Johnson as a mark of their appreciation of the prompt and courageous manner in which he arrested John Tiger on Christmas Day and also for his effective work in preserving the public peace during the excitement that followed the lamentable occurrences of that day. A man cannot be paid cash for this kind of work. Duty is all that prompts a man under such circumstances. This present to Grant is not, therefore, a reward but a mark of appreciation of duty well done, the reward for which is only the sense of duty well done.

On 6 September 1901 the same newspaper reported that Grant Johnson had killed another man in the line of duty. A recent quarrel between two Eufaula black men, Frank Wilson and Wade Smith, had led to Wilson firing two errant shots at the fleeing Smith. Wilson then fled himself, but Johnson gave chase on horseback. The marshal called for Wilson to stop and fired his revolver in the air in an effort to call for him to stop, but Wilson said he would rather die than surrender and levelled his pistol at Johnson. The marshal fired first, hitting Wilson in the belly. Wade Smith then suddenly appeared with a shotgun and would have shot the wounded Wilson while he lay on the ground, but Johnson intervened. Despite good medical attention, Wilson died the next day.

Grant Johnson also had a major role in the 1901 Crazy Snake Uprising. Disgruntled Creeks, full-bloods of the Snake faction as well as freedmen, led by the charismatic Chitto Harjo (Crazy Snake) sought to resurrect the sovereignty of the Creek Nation. The Snakes elected a principal chief and set up a new government. They began attacking the Creeks who willingly took land allotments, employed whites or rented land to outsiders, and that prompted the federal government to intercede. Grant Johnson had to arrest Harjo and some of his followers several times.

On 28 January 1901, the *Daily Herald* of Delphos, Ohio, reported on one such instance in which Grant Johnson, assisted by posseman Bunnie McIntosh, stormed a hostile Creek camp near Henrietta and arrested Harjo. The story said: 'The capture of the central figure of the uprising and the show of force which the troops will make will likely put an end to the threatened outbreak'.

However, tensions between the Crazy Snakes and the US Government continued until Grant Johnson once again led a posse into the Creek camp and arrested Harjo and 11 of his main followers, without any resistance.

In November 1904, Deputy US Marshal Ed Fink was murdered by two Indian outlaws by the name of Jim Tiger and Peter Fish, who had been apprehended trying to smuggle bootleg whisky into the Indian Territories. Immediately warrants were sworn out for their arrest and every US Deputy Marshal in the area was on the trail looking for them, including Grant Johnson and J.F. 'Bud' Ledbetter. Bud Ledbetter knew that Jim Tiger had relatives in Eufaula, all full-blood Snake Indians, which made him believe the pair had doubled back toward that town or some hideout near the point where the Deep Fork and South Canadian rivers met. Deputy US Marshal Bud Ledbetter, together with his horse, took the train from Muskogee to Eufaula, where he picked up Grant Johnson. The two lawmen searched the area and trails, and then at Mellette, 15 miles east of Eufaula, caught and arrested Tiger and Fish without resistance.

In July 1905 Johnson tracked down a murderer named Jonas McIntosh and then shot him dead when the outlaw resisted arrest. Meanwhile, Grant Johnson and Bud Ledbetter continued to work well together, with Johnson taking care of things in Eufaula and Ledbetter handling crime in the Muskogee area. Then a problem developed on 3 February 1906, when their boss, US Marshal Bennett, sent Ledbetter to Eufaula to investigate allegations about light alcoholic drinks being sold illegally in drugstores and gambling joints there. When Grant Johnson heard about this he was furious about Bud Ledbetter going into his territory without him knowing, so that same night he raided four craps games and arrested a dozen men in Muskogee, Ledbetter's district. The fact that Bud Ledbetter was just obeying orders from Bennett seemed to elude Grant Johnson, and probably Ledbetter himself queried why he was being sent to Eufaula instead of Grant Johnson.

Bud Ledbetter dismissed Johnson's action as nothing more than a minor disagreement, but on 9 February 1906 US Marshal Bennett told Johnson he that would not be reappointed as a Deputy US Marshal. It was a blow to Johnson, who took pride in his distinguished record over nearly 20 years as a federal lawman. He then became a police officer in Eufaula's black community and lived there until his death on 9 April 1927. 'Johnson, although a Negro, was a fearless, courageous officer and had many friends both among the coloured and white citizens of the state', the *Indian Journal* noted in its 14 April edition. 'He made a record in the early days of the Indian country and will go down in history as one of the best peace officers this section of the state ever had.

Deputy US Marshal Eli Hickman Bruner.

He was buried [at Evergreen Cemetery] here Wednesday'. More glowing words from an anonymous person came on 16 April:

The death of Grant Johnson brings my mind back 40 years ago when Grant was on the force. Grant was a Negro, but being a marshal did not give him the big head. He was brave, yet he was kind to his prisoners. He was on the force in the day of Belle Starr. When Younger Bend was the suburbs of hell, Grant would go in the Bend and hunt for outlaws. Without a doubt he was the best Negro that was ever on the force. Bass Reeves did a lot of service, but after all this he was mean to his men. Grant Johnson ranks first of the old US Marshals of the Negro race. Oklahoma Negroes should study his record as officer and citizen.

Grant Johnson was unquestionably one of the best lawmen of the Fort Smith federal court. But rating him better than Bass Reeves is a stretch. Nobody trying to uphold justice in Indian Territory could match Reeves. Still, Johnson was a true hero of the Old West. Maybe he wasn't the Lone Ranger, but there is nothing wrong with being Tonto.

Chapter 21

Paden Tolbert

Paden Tolbert was the eldest of eight children born to James Russell Tolbert and Elizabeth Miller and grew up in Griffin, Georgia during the Reconstruction era. His father James had graduated from the University of Georgia and had studied law in Tennessee before deciding to become a journalist. During the Civil War the family lived in Atlanta, while James Tolbert reported for the Atlanta Constitution. Prior to the American Civil war, the Tolbert family had enjoyed a comfortable life, but like many other families in the South had suffered as a result of the war. At the end of the war the family moved to Pike County and tried their hand at farming, but were unsuccessful. In 1880, his father sold the family estate in Griffin and travelled to Clarksville, Arkansas, where he decided to try his hand at growing peach trees, an enterprise at which he became very successful. He was later responsible for the introduction of the *Elberta* peach.

Deputy US Marshal Paden Tolbert.

Paden Tolbert decided that growing peaches was not for him and became a schoolmaster in Johnson County for a year before deciding on a career as a law enforcement officer. He travelled to Fort Smith and, at age 22, became one of the youngest Deputy US Marshals under 'Hanging Judge' Isaac Parker. Shortly after becoming a US Marshal, Paden Tolbert

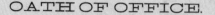

OATH OF OFFICE.

I, _Paden Tolbert_ .... do solemnly swear that I will faithfully execute all lawful precepts, directed to the Marshal of the United States for the Western District of Arkansas, under the authority of the United States, and true returns make and in all things well and truly, and without malice or partiality, perform the duties of Deputy Marshal of the Western District of Arkansas during my continuance in said office, and take only my lawful fees, so help me God.

Paden Tolbert (S. S.)

Sworn and subscribed to before me this _29th_ day of

_____ 189_3_

Clerk.

Paden Tolbert's Oath of Office, signed by Paden Tolbert and Judge Isaac Parker.

married his childhood sweetheart Lucy Rose Turner and moved to the Indian Territory. Later his brother John also became a Deputy US Marshal at Fort Smith and the two briefly worked together. Another deputy he was partnered with was Bud Ledbetter, who had a fearsome reputation for getting his man, and together over the coming years, they hunted down many notorious outlaws in the Indian Territory.

A well-armed Deputy Sheriff Bud Ledbetter.

One of the most notorious outlaws Paden Tolbert helped arrest was Ned Christie. Tolbert and Deputy US Marshal G.S. 'Cap' White led the 16-man posse that included Heck Thomas, Bud Ledbetter and Paden's brother John Tolbert, who searched the Indian Territory for Ned Christie.

Christie had a reputation for being one of the most vicious outlaws in Indian Territory. Dime novels at the time painted him as a born

Part of the posse that caught Ned Christie with a young Paden Tolbert on the far right.

Deputy US Marshals with Paden Tolber seated in the front holding a revolver.

killer, cold-blooded and ruthless with a maniacal hatred for white men. He was said to have murdered more than 11 people, though officially he was charged with only the one, and that was of US Deputy Marshal Daniel Maples. For five years Christie, who always maintained his

The charismatic outlaw Ned Christie.

innocence, had evaded the lawmen attempting to bring him in to stand trial for that murder.

Ned Christie's involvement started on the night of 5 May 1887 in downtown Tahlequah. Christie had met John Parris, a half-breed, who had been in trouble with the court in Fort Smith for years for introducing and selling whisky. He and Christie went to Dog Town on the northern edge of Tahlequah where they found a whisky peddler by the name of Bub Trainor and bought a bottle. In the meantime Deputy US Marshal Dan Maples had a warrant to arrest Trainor for selling whisky in the Indian Territory and, together with his posseman, George Jefferson, went looking for him.

The two deputies approached a wagon camp where Trainor, Parris and Ned Christie were drinking. As they approached the two men in the dark a shot rang out and Maples fell to the ground mortally wounded. The following morning Ned Christie, who claimed he had been so drunk that he was oblivious to all this, woke up to find that he was wanted for the murder of Deputy US Marshal Dan Maples. At first John Parris had been arrested for the murder, but he claimed that it was Ned Christie that had fired the shot. Realising that he had no way of proving his innocence, Ned Christie went on the run and for the next five years eluded the law.

Finally the law caught up with him and
on the morning of 2 November 1894, Paden
Tolbert and the rest of the posse surrounded
the near impregnable wooden fortress
known as the 'Rabbit Trap' in the Going
Snake District, a mountainous region of the
Cherokee nation (near present-day Talequah,
Oklahoma). Christie had successfully fought
off previous attempts to apprehend him for
well over a year before their arrival. While
the rest of the posse stocked up on extra
weapons including rifles, revolvers and
small-arms ammunition, Tolbert travelled
over 250 miles to Coffeeville, Kansas, and
brought back a military cannon from Fort
Knox that fired three-pound shells.

Dan Maples.

After cannon fire and over 2,000 bullets
had been fired at the double-tiered log
fortification and had proved ineffective, it seemed that more drastic
action would be required. As night fell, Tolbert and the others set to
work on building a portable shield. Using the charred rear axle and
wheels from the burned out lumber wagon used to assault the fort
the previous month, they built and mounted a thick wall from scrap-
oak timbers and loaded with rails. Sometime near midnight, Tolbert
helped push the wagon towards the cabin along with White, Charley
Copeland, Bill Ellis and Bill Smith. While Christie and his partner
attempted to fight off Paden's group from the second-storey gun ports,
the rest of the posse provided covering fire until the men were close
enough to plant six sticks of dynamite and breach the fort's walls and
the south wall of the house. Surviving the explosion, Christie made a
run for the surrounding woods but was gunned down by Paden Tolbert
and others.

Then, in 1896, a man called Richard Humphrey came forward and
said that he had witnessed the shooting of the Deputy US Marshal.
He claimed that he saw Ned Christie passed out on the ground and
Trainor take Ned Christie's jacket from him and put it over his white
shirt. Then Trainor stood behind a tree with a revolver in his hand
and fired into the darkness. Trainor then took off the jacket and threw
it over Ned Christie, who was still passed out. When asked why he
hadn't come forward before, Humphrey said that he was fearful of
Trainor and his friends, and it wasn't until he heard that Trainor had

Members of the posse who killed Ned Christie, with Christie's body propped up against the wall. Back row (left to right): Paden Talbot, Captain G. White, Ned Christie, Thomas Johnson, Coon Ratteree, Heck Bruner. Front row: Enoch Mills, Charles Copeland.

Some members of the posse that tracked and caught Ned Christie.

been killed that he decided to put the record straight. After a hearing Ned Christie was given a posthumous pardon.

Two years later, Paden Tolbert and several other US Marshals were contacted by the American Express Company, requesting protection because they had received information about a planned hold-up from one of their agents in Dallas. On 13 November 1894, Tolbert and Ledbetter were aboard the express car along with Sid Johnson, Frank Jones and as many as three Pinkerton detectives. The train was moving at top speed when Nathaniel 'Texas Jack' Reed and his gang stopped it. They called on the lawmen to get out of the express car, but Tolbert and the others refused to surrender and instead began firing at them. The gunfight continued for over an hour and a half until one of Reed's men, Charley Belstead, was killed. Reed then ran towards the passenger car, carrying dynamite with him, and tried to blow the express car. Failing in this attempt, he instead held up the passenger car. Erroneously reported killed as he and his men made their getaway, Reed was nevertheless wounded by Ledbetter. The failure of this attack resulted in a manhunt for the fugitives and the eventual capture of Reed.

Pinkerton detectives (Charles Siringo on left) on the trail of the Wild Bunch.

Charles Siringo with his pack horse about to leave.

In mid-July 1897, Paden Tolbert and Bud Ledbetter again rode together to bring in members of the Jennings Gang, brothers Alan and Frank Jennings. During their search, they learned that Al Jennings and

Nathaniel 'Texas Jack' Reed.

other parties were travelling about in the Northern District of the Indian Territory under assumed names. Paden Tolbert and Bud Ledbetter were sent after them with a warrant for their arrest after the robbery of a post office at Foyil in Cherokee territory. They stayed on their trail for some time before tracking them to the Spike S ranch and, along with several other Deputy US Marshals and possemen, surrounded the hideout. After a brief gunfight, in which the gang managed to escape, the federal officers chased them a distance of 60 miles before apprehending them together with Pat and Morris O'Malley.

On his release from prison, Al Jennings wrote a book about his life as an outlaw

142

Above left: Train robber Al Jennings. Photograph taken on his arrival at Levanworth Prison.

Above right: Poster advertising the films of Al Jennings and Vivian Gane.

and appeared in a couple of films before unsuccessfully entering the political arena. He appeared in a few films both as an actor and as a technical advisor.

After a successful 12-year career, Tolbert retired and became a special officer for Fort Smith and Western Railroad. After only a few months, he became ill with congestion of the lungs and was sent to Hot Springs, Arkansas, to recover. However, his condition did not improve and he died in Weleetka, Oklahoma, on 24 April 1904 and was buried in Oakland Cemetery near Clarksville, Arkansas, four days later. Following his death, his widow was appointed honorary postmistress of Paden, a town in the Indian Territory named after her husband.

Chapter 22

Ben Daniels

Benjamin Franklin 'Ben' Daniels was born on 4 November 1852, to Aaron Daniels and Mariah Sanders, but lost his mother, two brothers, and four sisters to cholera when he was still very young. Sometime in 1863 or 1864, when he was 11 years old, Ben moved with his father and stepmother to Kansas. By the age of 16 he was on his own, riding herds in Texas and later working as a buffalo hunter in Kansas. On 20 November 1879, in his late twenties, Ben Daniels was at Camp Carlin, Wyoming, when he was accused and convicted of stealing army mules. He was sentenced to three years and six months in the Wyoming Territorial Penitentiary as convict No.88.

Benjamin Franklin Daniels.

Ben Daniels was the perfect example of an outlaw turned lawman. On his release from prison on 28 August 1883 he headed for Dodge City, where he met and made friends with Bat Masterson and city marshal Bill Tilghman. When Bill Tilghman's assistant marshal, Tom Nixon, was killed by 'Mysterious Dave' Mather, Tilghman recommended that Ben Daniels be considered as a suitable replacement. Ben was duly appointed on 24 July 1884 at a salary of $100 a month. Daniels's two-year term as assistant marshal expired on 10 April 1886. With the money he had saved, he opened the Green Front Saloon in Dodge City. Ed Julian, the owner of a restaurant next door to the Green Front, began complaining about the noise and rowdy behaviour at Daniels's saloon. Within days Ben Daniels was ordered by town officials to close his saloon. Angered by the decision, Daniels went looking for Ed Julian and, when he found him, shot him in the back. The evidence clearly pointed to the shooting being murder, but somehow Daniels was acquitted. Immediately following the verdict, Daniels moved on.

On 6 March 1887, Ben Daniels married Laura 'Annie' Broaddus at Blue Springs, Missouri. They moved to Lamar, Bent County, Colorado, where Ben Daniels was offered and accepted an appointment as deputy sheriff of Bent County during January 1888.

In the late 1880s, the Gray County War erupted and Ben Daniels became involved. This was a dispute over the location of the Gray County seat in Western Kansas and Ben Daniels was one of the lawmen that participated in the gunfight in Cimarron on 12 January 1889.

The problem started when the new county clerk at Ingalls, the designated county seat, demanded all the county records be sent to him immediately. When the citizens at Cimarron refused to hand them over, the citizens of Ingalls organised a raiding party to go and take them by force if it became necessary. The party included Bill Tilghman, Jim Masterson, Ben Daniels, Fred Singer and Neal Brown, all former

Some of the 'mercenaries' hired in the Gray County War.

lawmen of Dodge City. They were assisted by 'mercenaries' Billy Allensworth, Ed Brooks and George Bolds. In order to make this legal, Bill Tilghman was sworn in as the temporary sheriff of Gray County, as the current sheriff, Joe Reynolds, was in hospital recovering from a gunshot wound. Bill Tilghman then swore all the raiding party in as deputy sheriffs of Gray County.

As the party were removing the county records, residents of Cimarron opened fire. Bill Tilghman was hit in the leg, George Bolds was hit in the leg and stomach and the wagon driver was hit in the arm, but despite their wounds they managed to clamber onto the wagon and leave town. The remaining members of the party were trapped inside the courthouse, where they started to return fire. After a six-hour battle the raiders surrendered to the townspeople of Cimarron with the promise that they would not be harmed. It transpired that someone had contacted Jim Masterson's brother, Bat, in Dodge City, (one can only assume by telegraph), to warn him that his brother was in danger. Bat Masterson is said to have sent the citizens of Cimarron a warning that if they didn't let his brother and his friends leave, he would hire a train and bring with him a party of gunfighters that would blow Cimarron off the face of the earth. Such was the reputation of Bat Masterson that the party was allowed to leave.

One man, John English, was killed during the fighting and seven others wounded. Three of the raiders were later charged with his

Old Gray County courthouse.

Main Street in Cimarron.

murder, but were acquitted after a short trial. The dispute continued until February 1893, when it was finally settled in a court of law and Cimarron became recognised as the county seat.

During 1893 Ben Daniels and his wife moved to the new boomtown of Cripple Creek, Colorado, where he pursued his gambling interests and performed occasional service as a lawman.

When the Spanish–American War broke out, 46-year-old Ben Daniels enlisted in Troop K of the 1st US Volunteer Cavalry, better known as the 'Rough Riders'. Ben was still living in Cripple Creek, where the local paper reported that, 'Ben Daniels left last night for San Antonio, Tex. He went as Cripple Creek's contribution to "Teddy's Terrors"', the cowboy regiment raised by Wood and Teddy Roosevelt.

Ben Daniels survived the famous battle for San Juan Hill, which took place during the war, and the more deadly malaria-carrying mosquitoes, to return to the state as a hero of what had been termed a 'splendid little war'. Ben was present at Camp Wikoff, Long Island, New York, on 15 September 1898 when Theodore Roosevelt and his Rough Riders were officially mustered out. When Theodore Roosevelt was asked about some of the Rough Riders by a newspaper he said:

'Some of our best recruits came from Colorado. One, a very large, hawk-eyed man, Benjamin Franklin Daniels, had been Marshal of Dodge City

147

when that pleasing town was probably the toughest abode of civilized man to be found anywhere on the continent. In the course of his rather lurid functions as peace officer he had lost half of one ear — 'bitten off,' as it was explained to me. Naturally he viewed the dangers of battle with philosophic calm. Such a man was, in reality, a veteran even in his first fight, and was a tower of strength to the recruits in his part of the line.'

After being discharged from the Rough Riders, Daniels began what was to become a 20-year correspondence with Theodore Roosevelt. After Roosevelt's appointment as President of the United States in September 1901, Ben Daniels wrote to him asking if the President could provide him with some sort of employment. On 8 January 1902 President Roosevelt appointed Ben Daniels as United States Marshal for the Territory of Arizona. That appointment was subject to confirmation by a majority of the United States' senate. The senate confirmed Daniels's appointment on 30 January 1902.

Within a week, Ben Daniels's appointment was subject to intense scrutiny by some of the people who had been opposed to his appointment. They found out about his prison record in Wyoming, and contacted the Attorney General of the United States. The story of his prison term had also been leaked to the press and within days telegrams and letters of complaint and praise poured into the White House. The pressure finally became too much for Roosevelt, and to save further problems for his friend, Ben Daniels submitted his resignation on 25 February 1902.

President Roosevelt was angered by the public outcry and remained determined to do something for Ben Daniels. He looked for something that wouldn't require senate confirmation to get one of his favourite Rough Riders on the federal payroll. He approached another former Rough Rider, Governor Alexander Brodie of Arizona, to appoint Daniels as superintendent of the Territorial Penitentiary at Yuma on 1 October 1904. Roosevelt wrote to his close friend, Senator Henry Cabot Lodge, saying:

'By the way, I think it will rejoice your heart to know that Governor Brodie of Arizona (late Lieutenant-Colonel of the Rough Riders) is going to appoint Ben Daniels (late one-eared hero of that organization) as warden of the Arizona Penitentiary. When I told this to John Hay he remarked (with brutal absence of feeling) that he believed the proverb ran: "Set a Rough Rider to catch a thief".'

Three years later, with the scandal caused by Theodore Roosevelt's first attempt to appoint Ben Daniels as US Marshal for Arizona largely forgotten, President Roosevelt finally appointed him, with the advice and consent of the senate, as the United States Marshal for the Territory of Arizona.

On 26 August 1906 Ben's wife, Annie Laura Daniels, died suddenly while visiting Ben's older sister, Elizabeth (Daniels) Copple, in Emporia, Kansas. She was buried at the cemetery in her family's hometown of Blue Springs, Missouri. Two years later Ben Daniels married for a second time. His new wife was a 39-year-old widow named Anna Evaline (Stakebake) Seayrs. His new bride, who preferred to be called 'Eva', was a schoolteacher who had a 10-year-old daughter by her first marriage.

Ben Daniels's past came back to haunt him after President Theodore Roosevelt left office in 1909, when he was called to Washington and asked to resign his commission as US Marshal for the Territory of Arizona. In a gesture of goodwill he was offered the position of Indian Agent at the Menominee Indian Agency in Green Bay, Wisconsin. Ben Daniels turned the offer down and returned to mining properties that he had in Arizona.

At the age of 62, Ben Daniels ran on Theodore Roosevelt's Progressive Party ticket for sheriff of Pima County, Arizona, and finished a very bad third. Two years later, again running on the Progressive ticket, he was again unsuccessful. After this second defeat, Ben then joined the Republican Party and in 1920, as a Republican, he was finally elected sheriff of Pima County. In May 1922, Daniels and his deputies investigated the robbery of the Golden State Limited train outside of Tucson and helped bring several of the culprits to justice in what was to be the last true train robbery in Arizona. Later that year, Daniels was defeated in a bid for re-election. The 70-year-old Daniels quietly went back to working his mining claims.

Ben Daniels died at 1.30 in the afternoon of 20 April 1923. He suffered a massive heart attack while he was seated in his parked automobile in Tucson.

Chapter 23

Dallas Stoudenmire

Dallas Stoudenmire was the epitome of the American Old West gunfighter and lawman, who gained fame for a brief gunfight that was later dubbed the 'Four Dead in Five Seconds Gunfight'.

Dallas Stoudenmire was born on 11 December 1845 in Aberfoil, Macon County, Alabama, one of nine children. Shortly after the American Civil War began, Dallas enlisted in the Confederate Army, even though he

was only 15 years old. He was over 6ft tall and well built, but when his senior officer discovered his age he was discharged. Records show that he re-enlisted twice more (the Civil War records show a Private D. Stoudenmire Company F of the 17th Alabama Infantry and a Private D. Stowdemire Company C, 6th Alabama Cavalry) and was eventually allowed to serve as a private in Company F, 45th Alabama Infantry Regiment. According to surviving records, he stood 6ft 4in tall by the war's end, was wounded a number of times and carried two bullets in his body for the remainder of his life.

After the war, Dallas Stoudenmire drifted west and served with the Texas Rangers for over three years. He acquired a reputation for being handsome, a sharp dresser and a ladies' man. But when drunk he could be extremely dangerous and had a violent temper. He became known for his habit of wearing two guns and being equally accurate

Dallas Stoudenmire.

with either hand. There is no record of him between 1874 and 1878, but he was possibly residing in Mexico for a time, as he was able to speak Spanish fairly well.

He next came to light while he was serving as the town marshal in Socorro, New Mexico. While employed there he had married Isabel Cummings. His brother-in-law and El Paso, Texas resident, Stanley 'Doc' Cummings, convinced him to take up a job as town marshal in El Paso. El Paso at that time was remote and almost lawless, and the city was seeking to hire a lawman with a 'tough reputation' to regain control. Dallas Stoudenmire travelled to El Paso to meet with the town council and was soon hired. This was the beginning of the end of a wild and violent El Paso, and Stoudenmire's rise to fame was set.

Dallas Stoudenmire became town marshal in El Paso on Monday 11 April 1881, facing a daunting challenge. He was the sixth town marshal in eight months. Immediately he was appointed, the city council asked him to take the city gaol keys from the deputy marshal, Bill Johnson, who was also well known as the town drunk. Witnesses stated that Dallas Stoudenmire had asked a drunk Johnson for the gaol keys. Johnson mumbled that he would go home and work out which keys were his and which were the town's. Dallas Stoudenmire became impatient and demanded he hand over the keys right away. When Johnson refused, Stoudenmire physically grabbed Johnson, turned him upside down, shook him until the keys dropped out of his pocket and then threw him to the ground in front of the local residents.

On Thursday 14 April 1881, only three days into his new job, Stoudenmire became involved in one of the most famous gunfights in Western history, called the 'Four Dead in Five Seconds Gunfight'. This gunfight made the headlines in newspapers in cities as far away as San Francisco and New York.

The events began a mile south, at the Rio Grande, which divided the United

Dallas Stoudenmire with two of his colleagues.

States and Mexico. On 14 April, the quiet of the late afternoon was shattered when 75 heavily armed Mexican cowboys galloped into El Paso looking for two missing young Mexican cowboys, named Sánchez and Jauregui, plus 30 cattle stolen from a ranch just across the river. The missing cattle belonged to a wealthy Mexican who had hired an armed posse to recover them. El Paso County Constable Gus Krempkau was asked by the leader of the Mexicans to lead them to a possible location. The bodies of the two missing Mexicans were discovered near Johnny Hale's ranch about 13 miles north-west of El Paso. Hale was a ranch owner and a known cattle rustler.

The bodies were taken back to town. It appeared that the two young Mexican cowboys were searching for the stolen cattle and had been trailing the herd when they were killed. Two cattle rustlers, Peveler and Stevenson, who worked for Johnny Hale, were overheard bragging about killing the two Mexican cowboys when they found them trailing the herd to Hale's ranch. They were arrested for the murder of the two young Mexican cowboys and brought before the court.

A large crowd gathered in El Paso, including John Hale and his friend, former town marshal George Campbell. There was a volatile tension in the air among the residents, worried about the dangerous presence of the large number of heavily armed and angry Mexicans who were demanding justice for the murdered men. Constable Gus Krempkau, who was fluent in Spanish, was required to interpret for the judge at the hearing being held in the court. The two rustlers were formally charged with the murders and were immediately placed under arrest. They were remanded in custody to stand trial at a later date. With the two rustlers now remanded to the local gaol, the court was adjourned and the crowd dispersed. The armed Mexicans, now having been assured by Marshal Dallas Stoudenmire and Constable Krempkau that justice would be done, calmed down and took the bodies of the two young Mexican cowboys back to Mexico for a proper burial.

The same evening, Constable Krempkau went into a saloon to retrieve his rifle and pistol, which he had left there prior to the hearing. A drunk and angry George Campbell confronted him over comments that Campbell was alleged to have said about Krempkau's interpreting in the court during the hearing and which showed bias toward the Mexicans. Also in the saloon was a very drunk John Hale, who was upset by Krempkau's role in the investigation and joined in the heated argument. Hale suddenly grabbed one of Campbell's two pistols and shot at Krempkau, hitting him in the chest.

Marshal Stoudenmire was eating dinner at a restaurant across the street when he heard the gunfire. He ran out with his gun in his hand,

and immediately started shooting in the direction of the saloon, killing an innocent Mexican bystander who was running for cover. Then, on entering the saloon, Stoudenmire shot at Hale, who was attempting to hide behind a pillar. Stoudenmire returned fire, killing him. When Campbell saw Hale drop dead, he tried to stop the fight. However, Krempkau, who was lying on the floor fatally wounded and believing that Campbell had shot him, fired at him twice before losing consciousness. The first of Krempkau's bullets struck Campbell's gun hand, which broke his wrist, causing him to drop the gun, while the second bullet struck his foot. Campbell screamed, but managed to scoop up his gun again. Stoudenmire, who was tending to Johnny Hale, whirled and fired, killing him. Constable Krempkau died later of his injuries.

The gunfight made Stoudenmire a legend, but it eventually had deadly consequences. Although his reputation as a gunman would continue to grow with later gunfights, he had few friends in El Paso, whereas both Campbell and Hale had many. Eventually, Stoudenmire would stand alone in his own defence of his actions. As was often the case, a shooting being proved justified meant very little in towns of the Old West, and vendettas were common.

Three days after the gunfight, on 17 April 1881, James Manning, a friend of both Hale and Campbell, persuaded former Deputy Marshal Bill Johnson to kill Stoudenmire. Johnson had an intense hatred of Stoudenmire for publicly humiliating him. That same night, a very drunk Johnson, stood behind a large pillar on the sidewalk with a loaded double-barrelled shotgun and waited. On hearing the voices of Stoudenmire and Stoudenmire's brother-in-law, Stanley 'Doc' Cummings, he raised the shotgun and as he did so staggered drunkenly and fell backwards, accidentally firing both barrels into the air. Stoudenmire quickly pulled out his pistols and fired at Johnson, severely wounding him. Johnson bled to death within a few minutes.

The death of Johnson started a feud between Stoudenmire and the Mannings. Within six days of his having started his job as town marshal, Stoudenmire had killed four men, one recklessly. Between the killing of Johnson and the following February, Stoudenmire killed another six men in shootouts during arrests and the city's crime rate dropped dramatically. His reputation, as both a lawman and a gunman, increased his legendary status.

On 14 February 1882, James Manning killed 'Doc' Cummings, claiming that he had acted in self-defence after an earlier argument that evening had escalated. Manning claimed that Cummings had pulled his pistol and verbally threatened to kill him outside the saloon. An innocent bystander walked by and Cummings turned and asked him if he was a friend of Manning's, to which the man said 'No!'. Cummings allowed him to go provided that he walked with his arms up in the air into the darkness of night. When Cummings turned back he realised that Manning had gone back inside the saloon. Cummings then entered the saloon and again threatened to kill him. Manning left the bar briefly and minutes later reappeared, armed with his pistols. Manning is said to have said, 'We will settle this for now and all'. In an instant, gunfire erupted from both sides. Hit, Cummings staggered out across a wooden sidewalk, toppling backward onto the dusty street as he screamed in agony then died.

Manning, who was uninjured, was acquitted after a 'trial', the jury finding that he had acted in self-defence. A large number of local residents and friends of the Mannings, some of whom had been members of the jury, attended the trial. The verdict enraged Stoudenmire and unfortunately for El Paso, Cummings had been the only man able to confront or control Stoudenmire's fierce temper. He publicly confronted those responsible for James Manning's acquittal and caused many to avoid coming into town or visiting saloons for fear of running into an enraged Stoudenmire.

Despite his prowess and his effectiveness as a lawman, Stoudenmire was an outsider. He was well respected by the Texas Rangers and the US Marshals, with whom he had worked on many occasions. However, he was not from El Paso, and had no family there other than his own family and his now deceased brother-in-law. The Mannings had been in El Paso longer and had many friends in the general population as well as in high places in the city council. Dallas Stoudenmire had two things in his favour; he had dramatically lowered El Paso's violent crime rate, more than any town marshal who came before him, and people truly feared him.

On 27 May 1882, the town council, after a great deal of pressure from Manning's friends, announced that Stoudenmire had been fired. Dallas Stoudenmire walked into the council hall drunk and dared them to take his guns or his job. The members of the council watched terrified as he pulled and twirled his guns and threatened to shoot them. They managed to calm him down by telling him he could keep his job. However, after sobering up he realised that he had made a fool of himself and resigned on 29 May 1882. He then became the owner of the Globe restaurant, which had formerly belonged to his brother-in-law Stanley Cummings. One month later US Marshal Harrington Lee 'Hal' Gosling approached Stoudenmire with an offer to become the Deputy US Marshal for Western Texas and New Mexico, a post he quickly accepted.

For a few months, Dallas Stoudenmire served well as a Deputy US Marshal. However, the feud was far from over. James Manning and his brothers, John 'Doc' Manning and Frank Manning, were careful to never confront Stoudenmire alone. Despite their hatred of him, he had shown his skill with a gun on several occasions and this made them wary. On one occasion, while standing out in the street, a drunken Stoudenmire mocked them, daring them to come outside and fight him. They remained inside a saloon while other residents attempted to convince Stoudenmire to go away and sleep it off. Eventually he grew tired, called the Mannings 'cowards', and left.

On 18 September 1882, the Mannings and Stoudenmire met in a local saloon, in an attempt to end the feud. James Manning, believing things were settled, left. Stoudenmire started off saying, 'Doc, someone or somebody has been going about telling lies'. Doc replied, 'Dallas, you have not kept your word.' 'Whoever says I have not, tells a damn lie,' replied Stoudenmire. With that Manning and Stoudenmire drew their pistols and fired. Stoudenmire's friend tried to push both men, causing Stoudenmire to lose his balance, and Doc's bullet hit Stoudenmire in his left arm. A second round hit Stoudenmire in the chest, but failed to even break the skin because of papers folded heavily in his shirt pocket. Nonetheless, the force of the second shot had knocked Stoudenmire down. As he fell outside the doorway, he pulled one of his pistols with his right hand and shot 'Doc' Manning in the arm. As Stoudenmire was firing, James Manning came from behind Stoudenmire and fired twice: one shot hit a barber's pole, while the other hit Stoudenmire behind the left ear, killing him. 'Doc' Manning then got up and started beating the dead man over the head with his own gun, before being restrained by James Manning.

The Mannings stood trial for the murder, but pleaded self-defence and were acquitted by a 'jury' made up mostly of their friends. They continued to live in El Paso, and soon the killing of Dallas Stoudenmire became just a memory. When Deputy City Marshal Thomas Moad was killed while investigating a disturbance at a local brothel on 11 July 1883, Frank Manning was appointed town marshal. Within months he had been replaced, as he often failed to arrest friends and acquaintances when they became involved in incidents.

A funeral ceremony for Stoudenmire was held at El Paso's Masonic Lodge #130. His wife Isabella then had his body shipped to Columbus, Texas, for burial. The Masonic Lodge paid for all funeral expenses and Dallas Stoudenmire was buried in the Alleyton Cemetery in Colorado County, Texas.

Chapter 24

'Mysterious' Dave Mather

David Allen Mather was born on 10 August 1851, the eldest of three brothers, the younger two being Josiah and George. Mather's father abandoned the family in 1856, and went back to sea. He was later murdered in Shanghai, China, aboard his ship the *Ellen,* on 13 September 1864. The news of his death did not reach Connecticut until two months later, when reports were printed in the Hartford press.

In 1860 David and Josiah went to live with their maternal grandfather, Josiah Wright, and by 1870 they were working as labourers and later living as boarders with a cousin. That same year, David and his brother Josiah,

'Mysterious' Dave Mather.

then aged 19 and 15, went to nearby Clinton, Connecticut, and signed on as part of the crew of a cargo ship, eventually making their way to New Orleans, where it is thought they went their separate ways. What happened to the other brother George is not known: one can only assume that he stayed with the cousin.

Dave Mather's exact whereabouts during his early years in the West are sketchy. It is known he was in Dodge City, Kansas, in 1872, where he and his brother Josiah are said to have reunited to become buffalo hunters. He was also rumoured to have partnered with Wyatt Earp in 1878 in a scheme to sell fake gold bricks in the town of Mobeetie, Texas, but there is no evidence to support this.

The first documented evidence of Mather's career came in 1879, when he was

156

recruited by Bat Masterson to serve in a posse to enforce the claims of the Atchison, Topeka and Santa Fe Railway during the Royal Gorge Railroad War. The posse was never called to action as the 'war' was settled in court.

Dave Mather moved to East Las Vegas, New Mexico, where he became a Deputy US Marshal for the Territory of New Mexico. In October 1879 he was arrested and tried for being involved in a train robbery, but after a short trial he was acquitted. He resigned as a Deputy US Marshal and joined the East Las Vegas police force.

It was in East Las Vegas that Dave Mather acquired his reputation as a gunman, when he got involved in a gunfight on 22 January 1880 while serving as deputy town marshal. He and Town Marshal Joe Carson were called to a disturbance at Close and Patterson's Variety Hall on Main Street, which resulted in a shootout with four men. In the ensuing gunfight Joe Carson was killed, then Mather killed one of the men, William Randall, and badly injured another, James West. He also wounded the other two, Thomas Jefferson House and John Dorsey, but their wounds were minor and they managed to flee the scene.

Now acting as town marshal, and just three days after the gunfight at Close and Patterson's Variety Hall, he was called to deal with another incident at the same establishment, this time with a disgruntled employee, Joseph Castello. In the heat of an argument with his employees, Castello had drawn his revolver and threatened to shoot them. When Dave Mather arrived at the Variety Hall, Castello pointed his weapon at Mather and warned him not to approach or he would shoot. It was said that Mather drew his weapon and fired a single lethal shot before Castello could return fire. At an inquest, the coroner's jury ruled that Mather's shooting was justifiable and carried out under the rule of self-defence.

Dave Mather's career as town marshal in east Las Vegas was short-lived. In February 1880, House and Dorsey, the two men who had escaped during the gunfight in which Town Marshal Joe Carson was killed, were captured and returned to the San Miguel county gaol. That same evening, an irate lynch mob broke into the gaol, 'overpowered' Dave Mather, dragged the two men and their fellow gunman James West out of gaol and hanged them. During the next month, there were two murders on the same day, both connected to one of the gambling house bosses. There were no arrests and the public began to suspect Mather had ties to the town mob boss as he was seen to frequent his establishment regularly. Mather realised that he was walking a thin line and resigned on 3 March 1880.

During his time in East Las Vegas, he had acquired the name of 'Mysterious' Dave Mather, mainly because he was a loner and nobody knew anything about him or his past. He did not leave East Las Vegas immediately and records show that he was still there as late as 19 March 1880, when he signed his name to a court document intended to help John Joshua Webb, who had been charged with murder.

For the next few years Mysterious Dave drifted around Texas having various minor skirmishes with the law, including a short time in a Texas gaol for counterfeiting. This was followed by a three-month term on remand in a Dallas gaol awaiting trial on charges of stealing a silk dress from a woman named Georgia Morgan with whom he had operated a brothel. He also faced three separate counts of theft of two diamond rings and a watch from Georgia Morgan. After a short trial Dave Mather was acquitted of all three charges on 13 April 1882.

Because of his previous experience as a town marshal, Dave was hired as an assistant city marshal in Dodge City in June 1882. He was replaced, after serving only nine months, by Tom Nixon. This created a feud between the two men. In the meantime Mather had opened a saloon and dance hall called the Opera House Saloon. The feud between Mather and Nixon was further fuelled when the city passed 'Ordinance No.83', outlawing dance halls within Dodge City. The ordinance was enforced against Mather's Opera House Saloon, preventing it from operating as a dance hall, but not against the Lady Gay Saloon, which was owned by Tom Nixon, which also featured dancing. In retaliation, Mather began a price war on beer. He charged only five cents a glass, half the price of his competitors. Nixon and the other Dodge City saloon owners pressurised the beer wholesalers to cut off Mather's supply, but to no avail. On 18 July 1884, the feud erupted into a shootout between the two when Nixon shot Mather, but only wounded him slightly. Tom Nixon immediately brought charges of attempted murder against Dave Mather. The feud erupted again three days later when Nixon again confronted Mather, only this time Tom Nixon was shot dead.

Despite witnesses, including Bat Masterson and Sheriff Patrick Sughrue, who said that Mather had acted in self-defence, Dave Mather was sent for trial accused of murder. The trial was moved to Ford County and lasted just three days. After hearing overwhelming evidence that Tom Nixon had been the aggressor throughout, the jury took just seven minutes to find Mather not guilty. Many regarded the verdict as a proper one and that David Mather had been justified in shooting dead Tom Nixon.

Early in 1885, Dave Mather's brother Josiah joined him in Dodge City. Trouble erupted again for Dave Mather on 10 May 1885 when he got into an argument with a man named David Barnes during a card game in which Josiah was also involved. Within seconds the argument had escalated and was followed by a gunshot, and Dave Barnes fell dead. Sheriff Patrick Sughrue arrested both brothers for murder. During the coroner's hearing, the jury heard evidence from Sheriff Sughrue that Dave Mather's gun was loaded and there were no empty shells in it. The jury was not convinced and stated that there could only have been two people involved in the death of David Barnes and they were the two Mather brothers. The jury came to the conclusion that David Barnes had died from a gunshot wound that could have only come from either Dave Mather or his brother Josiah Mather, and so they were bound over for trial.

After a hearing before Judge Strang on 2 June 1885, the two brothers were allowed bail on a bond of $3,000. After a number of legal arguments their respective lawyers got the trial date set for the beginning of December. The trial never happened because the two defendants jumped bail and disappeared.

What happened to Mysterious Dave Mather after this is not known, although there were reports that he became town marshal of New Kiowa, Kansa, for a short time, but had to leave after an incident concerning a friend of his, Dave Black. Black had shot and killed a young soldier, a bugler by the name of Julius Schmitz from the 18th Infantry Regiment of the Union Army. Dave Mather had raised over $300 for his friend's defence fund, but then heard that soldiers from the young bugler's company were planning to come after him for helping the killer of one of their soldiers. Realising that he was in serious trouble and would get no support from anyone, as there was anger surrounding the killing of the young man, he decided to leave.

The last time anyone heard of Mysterious Dave Mather was when it was reported that he had joined the Royal Canadian Mounted Police in the Northwest Territories and had robbed a stage he was supposed to be guarding and had got away with $20,000. The Royal Canadian Mounted Police said that they had no record of anyone with that name joining the RCMP. His brother Josiah later said that his brother had been killed by 'Moonshiners', but this is contradicted by his children, who said that they were told by their father that he had never seen or heard from his brother after the incident in Dodge City.

Chapter 25

Frank Canton

Frank Canton was another enigma, inasmuch as he was both lawman and outlaw. He was born Josiah Horner on 15 September 1849 in Harrison Township, Henry County, Indiana, and in his late teens drifted into Texas, working as a cowboy on various ranches. In 1871, tired of riding herds, he started robbing banks and rustling cattle, which was a capital offence. On 10 October 1874 Horner got into a gunfight with some Buffalo soldiers, killing one and wounding the other. What happened concerning this incident is not known. Three years later Texas Rangers arrested him for robbing a bank in Comanche, Texas. He escaped from their custody and fled to Ogallala, Nebraska, where he changed his name to Frank Canton and took up ranching.

Little is known about him during the next few years, but in 1884 he appeared in Wyoming as a stock detective for the Wyoming Stock Growers Association. He was also a Deputy US Marshal at a time of escalating tension between the wealthy cattlemen and the ever-increasing population of homesteaders, who were by sheer numbers putting an end to free ranging and altering the balance of political power. This tension rapidly escalated into what became the Johnson County War.

Frank Canton was elected sheriff of Johnson County in 1885, and was seen as the legal enforcer for the cattle barons. He served for four years, but was forced to resign after the foreman of the one of the big ranches, who had been arrested on suspicion of murder, escaped under questionable circumstances while in his custody. Although still working part-time as a US Deputy Marshal, rumours started to circulate that Canton was also an assassin and enforcer for the wealthy ranchers. Things came to a head when, during an investigation into the death of a law-abiding homesteader, it was discovered that the life of the homesteader had been threatened by Frank Canton. The homesteader had told Frank Canton that he had evidence against some of Canton's friends, implicating them in an earlier murder. When the other homesteader heard of this a lynch mob was formed and Canton was arrested for his own protection and further investigation. Several of the big ranchers stood surety for him and his lawyer got him released. He immediately left the state and headed for Illinois. By the time further evidence against him was found, pressure from the wealthy ranch-owners forced the matter to be dropped.

During the Johnson County War, Canton had drawn up a list of rustlers who were instrumental in taking advantage of the war and robbing the ranchers of their cattle. On 9 April 1892, Canton was hired by the ranchers to lead a group of hired gunmen called the 'Regulators'. Canton led them to the KC Ranch, where number one on the list, Nate Champion, lived.He had also been a witness against some of Canton's friends for a murder. Staying with Champion was Nick Ray, who was shot and killed in the opening minutes of the ensuing gun battle. The 'Regulators' suffered many casualties in the gunfight: at least four were killed and a number were wounded. In a desperate effort to finish the fight Canton set the house on fire. Nate Champion burst out of the house firing his Winchester rifle against impossible odds and was shot 28 times. The 'Regulators' went to the TA Ranch to regroup, but two days later a huge posse, led by Sheriff Angus, surrounded the ranch house calling for them to surrender. Fortunately for Canton and his 'Regulators' the US Cavalry arrived to intervene. The newspapers, heavily influenced and controlled by the powerful cattle barons, portrayed the 'Regulators' in a

Studio portrait shot of Frank M. Canton.

favourable light, saying that they were ridding the state of rustlers and outlaws. Canton and the other regulators were freed. Canton decided that it was time to leave Wyoming and headed for Arkansas.

Frank Canton still held the position as a Deputy US Marshal and on reaching Fort Smith offered his services. Over the next couple of years Canton rode with some of the most famous lawmen in the Indian Territories: Bass Reeves, Chris Madsen, Bill Tilghman and Heck Thomas. In one incident Frank Canton joined as a posseman with Bill Tilghman and tracked down two desperate outlaws, brothers Bill and John Shelley, who had numerous warrants out for their arrest. They had escaped from the Pawnee gaol and had barricaded themselves in a log cabin on the banks of the Arkansas River. A five-hour gun battle ensued in which countless shots were fired. Frank Canton decided that the only way they were going to resolve this was to set fire to the cabin and force them to surrender. Loading up an old wagon with dry brushwood he set it alight and sent it into the cabin. Minutes later the two brothers surrendered and were taken into custody.

On another occasion, Frank Canton was in Pawnee, Oklahoma armed with a warrant for a man called Bill Dunn. On 6 November Canton confronted Bill Dunn in the street and told him that he had a warrant for his arrest. Canton's description of the incident, if true, was like something out of a Western film. He said Bill Dunn shouted at him,

Above: Chris Madsen when a member of Roosevelt's 'Rough Riders'.

Left: Frank M. Canton.

'Damn you, Canton. I've got it in for you!' He then reached for his pistol, which got caught in his trouser braces. Canton drew and fired, hitting Dunn in the head and killing him instantly. The local sheriff accepted, after hearing from witnesses, that Canton had acted lawfully and in self-defence.

Canton continued his work as a Deputy US Marshal, but it ended in disputed circumstances with accusations that he had misused public money. The following year in 1897, Canton went to Alaska to follow the gold rush in the Klondike. After 10 unsuccessful years in the Alaskan wilderness Frank Canton returned to the United States, and in 1907 became adjutant general for the Oklahoma National Guard. It was around this time that

Frank M. Canton, lawman turned outlaw.

Frank Canton confessed to the governor of Texas that he was in fact Josiah Horner and was a wanted man. The governor, Thomas Mitchell Campbell, took into consideration his time as a US Deputy Marshal and granted him a pardon. Canton died on 27 September 1927 in Edmond, Oklahoma.

Chapter 26

Floyd Wilson

One of the most respected Deputy US Marshals who worked out of Fort Smith federal court during the 1880s and 1890s was Floyd Wilson. He also worked on and off as a town lawman in Fort Smith, Arkansas, yet sadly today he is remembered for the fact that he was the one and only person killed by the infamous Cherokee Indian bank robber Henry Starr.

Floyd Wilson was born Floyd Alderman Wilson on 9 May 1860 in Lee Township, Athens County, Ohio. He attended just one term of college at St Mary's College in Emmittsburg, Maryland, before deciding to enlist in the US Army. For the next five years, from 1878 to 1883, he served in Texas and the Indian Territory.

Deputy US Marshal Floyd Wilson.

On leaving the army Floyd Wilson worked for some months with Deputy US Marshal Bass Reeves as a posseman in the Chickasaw Nation. Then, on 5 January 1884, Floyd Wilson received a commission as a Deputy US Marshal for the Western District of Arkansas. There is also a document showing that Wilson received a further commission on 22 October 1889. Floyd Wilson continued to work with Bass Reeves, who by the time of Wilson's commission had served almost 10 years as a deputy for the Fort Smith court. He helped to train Wilson in the art of being a field Deputy US Marshal, something he did for other young deputies new to the court and territory.

Deputy US Marshal Floyd Wilson's Oath of Office.

Soon after joining with Reeves they had a warrant for the arrest of Jim Webb, the foreman of the Washington-McLish Ranch. Webb had murdered a black man named Reverend Stewart who owned a small farm next to the huge Washington ranch. Stewart had inadvertently started a fire that got out of control and burned a large portion of the grazing land on the Washington spread. Webb, who had a violent temper and was not known for his tolerance, confronted Stewart in regards to the fire and, after a heated argument, shot him dead.

Reeves and Wilson rode onto the Washington ranch disguised as cowboys looking for work. They were met by foreman Jim Webb and a cowboy by the name of Frank Smith who, with pistols in their hands, initially regarded them with some suspicion. Bass Reeves managed to convince them that he and Floyd Wilson were just looking for work and nothing else. They were invited to have breakfast, but Bass Reeves noted that the two men still did not appear to be convinced, as they were kept under their watchful eye. After eating breakfast Bass Reeves got into a conversation with Webb, while Floyd Wilson kept an eye on Frank Smith. Then something in the yard distracted Webb and, as he looked away, Reeves leapt forward, drawing his pistol as he did so, and grabbed Webb by the throat. The movement was so quick that Floyd Wilson barely had time to react. Frank Smith pulled out his gun in an attempt to shoot Reeves, but missed. Bass Reeves returned fire, mortally wounding Smith while still holding Webb by the throat. Webb was arrested for murder and later hanged. Frank Smith was buried near Tishomingo, Johnson County, Oklahoma.

The two US Marshals continued to work together on a number of occasions, but Floyd Wilson was becoming more and more experienced, which was highlighted in a newspaper report in the *Fort Smith Elevator* on 15 February 1884:

> *Deputy Floyd Wilson reported on Friday last with eleven prisoners, as follows: Lewis Sanders and Charles Buffington (Negroes) William and Ed Bait, Thos. McDaniel and Albert Scraper (Indians), and William Columbus (white) charged with introducing whisky in the Territory; James Lee (Indian), George Vann, Levi and William Steel (white), larceny. McDaniel gave bond and the balance were locked up.*

In March 1884 Wilson was again acting as posseman for Deputy US Marshal Bass Reeves, along with William Leach as cook, and John Brady as guard, when they left Fort Smith for the Indian Territory to collect 12 prisoners. During this trip into the territory it was said that Bass Reeves accidentally shot Leach while trying to eject a jammed cartridge from his rifle. Floyd Wilson was not present when the shooting incident occurred. Because there were some doubts about Reeves's explanation, he was arrested for first-degree murder in 1886 for shooting Leach and suspended from duty. In October 1887, Reeves was acquitted by a jury after a trial and returned to work as a Deputy US Marshal, a position he was to hold until 16 November 1907.

The *Fort Smith Elevator* reported on that trip into the territory:

> *Deputies Reeves and Wilson came in Wednesday with the following prisoners: James Geeson, assault with the intent to kill; Eleck Bruner, Aaron Sancho and Hotablsy, larceny; Crotsey Fixico, Tobey Hill, Golmo Jessee, Wiley Hawkins, Noah, Charley Jones, Amos Hill and G. H. Brewer, introducing liquors. One of their prisoners who was severely wounded*

while resisting arrest had to be left in the Territory, a physician saying that to move him would endanger his life.

There is no record of any of the prisoners being severely wounded, so it was almost certain that it was William Leach the cook and not a prisoner who was the wounded party.

On 25 February 1886 Floyd Wilson married Bridget Kelly in Fort Smith, Arkansas. The Kelly family had come from Ireland to New Orleans and then by steamboat up the Mississippi and Arkansas rivers to Fort Smith in around 1855. The Wilsons early married life was spent in Vinita, in the Cherokee Nation, and Muskogee, in the Creek Nation, before they moved back to Fort Smith in March 1887.

In March 1886 Floyd Wilson and posseman Sam Wingo captured and arrested a couple of notorious outlaws. The *Fort Smith Elevator* reported:

Newt Scrempsher and Charlie Counter, brought in a few days ago by Floyd Wilson and Sam Wingo on charges of murder have not yet been examined by the Commissioner. Newt is charged with the murder of a man named Secrest in 1879. Counter, who also answers to the name of Grunter, is a Seminole and is said to have murdered a white man named Holleren about seven years ago near Okmulgee. Holleren was murdered while engaged in hauling corn, his slayer having first shot him and then drove his team into the woods where he dumped him out of the wagon and left the team and wagon there. If Counter can't prove hi is not the man that did it he is in a bad box. Scrimpsher (sic) has lived at Muskogee for several years, during which time he has been a law abiding citizen, though at one time he was quite bad, being associate of the notorious Jim Barker, and has been before the courts on more than one occasion for acts of lawlessness.

At the beginning of 1887, tired of being away from his wife and family for long periods of time, Floyd Wilson left the US Marshal service and took a job as a Fort Smith police officer. By the end of the year he had been promoted to sergeant. During this period, Floyd Wilson and Captain Henry Surratt arrested two black men, Martin Council and Harvey Blackburn, for a burglary of the D. Baker & Co. merchandise store and the theft of 300 dollars' worth of clothing, jewellery and other items. After much searching the two officers were able to retrieve just 50 dollars' worth of goods in a damaged condition. They later found considerably more stolen merchandise hidden in the loft of the local Episcopal Church.

Then, in January 1889, the mayor removed Floyd Wilson, together with Captain Henry Surratt, city detective Wiley Cox and John McDaniel from the Fort Smith police department. These men were the most senior men on the department and this caused major problems within the police force itself. It resulted in inexperienced policemen having to be brought in to the city to maintain law and order. The local newspaper followed up on the story, saying that they believed it was because the four men had signed a petition in support of a local man who was an applicant for the postmaster's job, which the mayor had also applied for. When the city council heard of this accusation they were appalled by the suspensions and the matter was referred to the city police committee. The four men were reinstated and returned to duty. Some months later, Wilson, tired of the political infighting that was affecting the police force, reapplied for the position of Deputy US Marshal at Fort Smith federal court.

Floyd Wilson was soon back in the saddle arresting wanted felons and in February 1890, he arrested a burglar named Burt Davis. The following month he arrested a notorious Creek Indian outlaw named Gibson Partridge, who was charged with murder, assault with intent to kill, larceny and a number of other offences. Wilson and his posse had been tracking Partridge for some time and finally caught up with him 28 miles from Tulsa, after a week-long chase. Partridge had been dodging the federal officers for about two years, stealing horses and committing other serious crimes. Floyd Wilson and his posse discovered Partridge hiding in the cabin of an Indian medicine man known as Old Caesar after a tip-off. The posse surrounded the cabin and called for Partridge to surrender, but he refused to come out. The posse told him that they would set fire to the cabin if necessary and once again he refused. Inside the house were some women and children and so they were allowed to leave the cabin before it was set on fire. The wooden cabin was soon engulfed in flames and just as the roof was falling in Gibson Partridge emerged. Coming to the door, he threw down his weapon and surrendered. He was immediately arrested. He was one of the last members of the notorious Wesley Barnett gang and had been tried for murder three times under the Creek Nation laws, once for the murder of his own brother. Gibson Partridge was later hanged.

During March 1890, Floyd Wilson continued maintaining law and order within the Indian Territory and arrested Sherman Westmoreland for violating postal law and a black man named William Garvin for stealing 1,500lb of flour from a freight car in the town of Cherokee. In the same year he arrested Star Wady, Sam B. Carter and John Wallace for selling whisky, and Richard Payne for assault, all in the Indian Territory.

On 2 May 1890, the Fort Smith Elevator reported on arrests made by Wilson:

> *Joe Banks, Adam Banks, and Annie King charged jointly with murder, and Eugene Lawther, charged with introducing, etc. were brought in Saturday by Deputy Floyd Wilson. The two Banks' and the King woman are Negroes, and they are charged with the killing of Annie's husband, who mysteriously disappeared in June last, and whose body was afterward found in a creek near his house. Adam Banks, who is a son of Joe, married King's step-daughter after the disappearance of King, and it is intimated that Joe Banks, the old man, wanted the widow, and for this reason they conspired to get King out of the way.*

One of the most interesting historical episodes in Floyd Wilson's law enforcement career concerned the infamous Dalton brothers. The oldest of the Daltons was Frank Dalton, who was commissioned as a Deputy US Marshal for the Fort Smith federal court and was killed in the line of duty. His three brothers, Bob, Grat, and Emmett, also worked in law enforcement. Bob Dalton had held a commission as Deputy US marshal for the Wichita federal court and chief of police for the Osage Indian Nation. All three, at one time or another, worked as possemen with Floyd Wilson just before becoming outlaws themselves. Near Vinita in February 1890, Grat Dalton assisted in arresting a Missouri Pacific Railroad foreman who was charged with beating an employee almost to death with a shovel. The accused was delivered to the Muskogee court for trial and later sentenced to a lengthy term of imprisonment. Emmett and Bob rode with Floyd Wilson in April 1890, when they captured Carroll Collier and Bud Maxfield near Claremore, Cherokee Nation. Both were escaped convicts from the Little Rock, Arkansas, penitentiary. There was a reward of $100 each for Collier and Maxwell, who were notorious horse thieves. In June 1890, the three Dalton brothers made their last trip with Floyd Wilson, when, after they had been paid for their services as possemen, they rode into the Osage country, where they stole 17 horses and a pair of mules that belonged to Clem Rogers. From this incident the Daltons got involved in numerous criminal activities, far too many to mention here, which ended two years later in Coffeyville, Kansas in October 1892.

Floyd Wilson continued to come to the attention of the local newspaper when, on 4 July 1890, the *Fort Smith Elevator* reported:

MAXFIELD IDENTIFIED
Mr. George Shannon, of Gibson Station, came down Monday to take a look at Eugene Standley, believing that he was one of three men who robbed him on the night of January 5th last. He could not fully identify Standley, but thinks he was one of the party. He did, however, positively identify, Bud Maxfield as the man who held the gun on him while he was opening the safe, and who repeatedly threatened to kill him. Maxfield denies being the man, but Shannon was so positive in his identification that he told Deputy Floyd Wilson, who captured Maxfield, to call at any time and get the $50 reward, he having offered that amount each for the robbers. The other two men who were with Maxfield were probably George Meyers and Jim Hullum, who escaped from the pen at the same time Maxfield and Carroll Collier did…

In the last week of July 1890, Floyd Wilson brought in Dave McDaniel, charged with horse stealing; Henry Hightman, charged with adultery and violating revenue law; Dan Hawes, assault with intent to kill, and William Dale, introducing and selling liquor in Indian Territory. Dave McDaniel was turned over to the Cherokee authorities, because he was a citizen of the Cherokee Nation and stole horses from Cherokees. The federal government only had jurisdiction when someone was a non-citizen and committed crimes against Indians or vice versa. Hightman was discharged and Hawes given a bond.

The *Fort Smith Elevator* reported on 15 August that Wilson had brought in from the Cherokee country David Ross, charged with assault, and George Denver and Dedrick Smith, for introducing illegal whisky into the Indian Territory. It is interesting to note that Floyd Wilson seems to have spent most of his career as a Deputy US Marshal working within the Cherokee Nation. Floyd Wilson also appears to have been the mainstay of supplying crime information for the *Fort Smith Elevator*.

In September 1890 Floyd Wilson was busy rounding up a number of individuals who had been committing crimes in the nearby territories. Among these was W.H. Spellman for larceny, who was arrested in the Oklahoma Territory, and Clabone C. Jones who was arrested for selling illegal whisky.

One person who remembered working with Floyd Wilson was the famous Wells Fargo detective Fred Dodge. They had worked closely together during a spate of train robberies in the Indian and Oklahoma territories.

Their first encounter was on 13 June 1891 at a home owned by a family called the Westmorelands in the Indian Territory. Fred Dodge, who had been investigating the disappearance of a number of men, was supposed to rendezvous with a posse led by Deputy US Marshal Heck Thomas. After spending the night with the family of Westmorelands, Dodge became concerned about their behaviour and, after spending an uneasy night, he was pleased to see Floyd Wilson arrive on the scene at daybreak with a posse. Wilson immediately arrested the Westmorelands on suspicion of murder, shortly after Heck Thomas and his posse arrived.

An early photograph of Fred Dodge as an undercover Wells Fargo detective.

The posses then investigated a nearby cave on the banks of the Arkansas River after reports by neighbours who had seen the Westmorelands carry something inside. Inside the posse found three skulls and skeletons; there was positive identification for two more men. Also found was evidence of four or five more men who had disappeared in the immediate vicinity. The Westmorelands, four men and an old lady, were taken to Fort Smith and, after a lengthy hearing, the four men were convicted and sentenced to hang, whilethe old lady got a life sentence at the US Penitentiary in Atlanta, Georgia.

Fred Dodge said that while he was in the Indian Territories he worked with Deputy US Marshals Heck Thomas, George Thornton, Bill Tilghman, Ed Short, Chris Madsen and Floyd Wilson. Then, in August 1892, Fred Dodge received a tip that nine heavily armed men were going to rob a San Frisco train at a tunnel near Winslow, Arkansas. After a conference with the railroad superintendent and US Marshal Yoes at Fort Smith, Floyd Wilson was tasked to investigate. Wilson assembled a posse consisting of Paden Tolbert and Bud Ledbetter, along with Dodge. The four men travelled to Winslow on a special train out of Fort Smith, but when they arrived at the tunnel they found out that the men were nothing more than a large hunting party, most of whom were known to Wilson, Tolbert and Ledbetter. The watchman, who tipped off Fred Dodge, said that he thought they were outlaws and was hoping to get a large reward. Tolbert and Bud Ledbetter were later hired by Fred Dodge to serve as Wells Fargo guards on trains running through the Indian Territory.

In the meantime Floyd Wilson's tenure as a Deputy US Marshal had come to an end. He reapplied for a position with the Fort Smith Police Department, which was immediately accepted. It was while with the police department that Deputy US Marshal and Pacific Express Company Detective Henry C. Dickey approached him. Dickey informed him that he had a warrant for the arrest of a Cherokee Indian by the name of Henry Starr, and he needed the expertise and experience of someone who knew the Indian Territory well, and Floyd Wilson was just that man. Floyd Wilson agreed to serve as Dickey's posseman and was reappointed a Deputy US Marshal, and together they set out for the northern part of the Cherokee Nation.

Henry Starr had been very busy in the Indian Territory. He had been arrested for horse theft in December 1891, and had failed to appear in court, resulting in the arrest warrant.

Henry Starr standing outside the gaol at Chandler, Oklahoma.

He was also suspected of robbing the Nowata, Cherokee Nation, railway depot of $1,700, followed by hold-ups of the Shufeldt's Store in Lenapah and Carter's Store in Sequoyah in November 1892, both in the Cherokee Nation. Starr had an additional horse theft warrant issued for his arrest on 18 November 1892.

On Monday 12 December, Hickey and Wilson rode up to Arthur Dodge's XU Ranch, located eight miles from Nowata. The deputies asked Dodge if he had seen Starr, to which he replied that he hadn't. Hickey and Wilson searched the nearby vicinity for the rest of the day without result. The following day the lawmen returned to the XU Ranch and were having dinner in the bunkhouse when Arthur Dodge rode up and said he had just seen Henry Starr riding by, pointing out the direction Starr had

172

taken. The two lawmen ran to the corral for their horses. Floyd Wilson's horse was already saddled and ready, so he jumped into the saddle and headed after Starr. Henry Dickey had to saddle his horse, putting him several minutes behind Wilson. Floyd Wilson caught up with Starr on the banks of Wolf Creek and called for him to stop, shouting that he had a warrant for his arrest. Henry Starr, holding his Winchester rifle across his saddle, stopped his horse and turned around. He told Floyd Wilson to 'Hold up' and, still holding his Winchester rifle, dismounted as Wilson closed to within 25 feet of him. Wilson, holding his own Winchester rifle, shouted that he was a federal officer and leapt from his horse and fired a warning shot over Starr's head. He hoped that this would encourage Starr to surrender, but instead of surrendering Henry Starr levelled his Winchester and fired several shots, knocking Floyd Wilson to the ground. Wilson managed to raise himself into a sitting position, jerked his pistol from its holster and fired four times, missing with all four shots. Henry Starr then ran up to Wilson, who was now lying on the ground, and fired point blank into the lawman's chest, killing him instantly. It was later discovered that there were powder burns on Wilson's coat and five bullet holes in the body. Wilson had been shot in the left hip, right hip, left thigh, left lower leg and once in the chest.

Around this time Henry Dickey arrived, and on seeing his colleague lying dead on the ground he dismounted and opened fire on Henry Starr. Starr returned fired at Dickey, then picked up Floyd Wilson's rifle and found the eject lever out of order. As he turned to walk away, Dickey, who was hugging the ground, fired at him but missed. In another exchange of gunfire, both Dickey's and Starr's horses ran away, but Starr managed to catch Floyd Wilson's horse, jumped into the saddle and rode off. Henry Starr's story is told in the companion volume *Outlaws and Bandits in the West*.

Deputy US Marshal Floyd Wilson was just 28 years old when he died and was the perfect example of 'true grit'. He was considered one of the best lawmen to ever work for the Fort Smith federal court under the jurisdiction of Isaac C. Parker. Without men like Wilson there would have been no law in the Indian Territory. Wilson's body was brought back to Fort Smith. Judge Isaac Parker immediately issued a warrant for the arrest of Henry Starr for the murder of a federal Deputy US Marshal and a massive manhunt was started.

Due to the fact he was an US Army veteran, Wilson was buried in the Fort Smith National Cemetery. The commitment made by this courageous lawman to bring law and order to the western frontier was second to none.

Chapter 27

Jeff Davis Milton

One of the most remarkable lawmen of the West was Jeff Davis Milton. Born in 1861 into a wealthy southern Florida family, his father was the Governor of Florida, General John Milton. Jeff Milton's career as a law enforcement officer was to span over 50 years. He was just three years old when the American Civil War ended and the reconstruction that followed had a dramatic effect on the family's Sylvannia estate. Then his father died due to an accidental gunshot wound. There was much speculation that he had committed suicide, but after an intense investigation it was accepted that it had been an accident.

Former Texas Ranger and Arizona lawman Jeff Milton.

With the demise of the estate and the family fortune, Jeff Milton was forced to find work and at the age of 15 briefly joined a mercantile company owned by a relative, before leaving and becoming a cowboy. Three years later he went to Austin, Texas and applied to join the Texas Rangers, telling them that he was 21 years old. He obviously looked much older than he was because they accepted him without question and he was sworn in as a private in the Texas Rangers. In these early days Texas Rangers had to provide their own firearms and usually chose a single action Colt .45 and an 1873 .44 Winchester rifle. The state initially supplied each Ranger with 100 cartridges then issued them with 12 rifle and six pistol cartridges per month thereafter.

174

Jeff Milton's first pistol was a nickel-plated .44-40 Colt, the same calibre as his rifle. But the first time he fired the pistol the cylinder jammed and it subsequently did so after every shot. He swapped it for a rather ornate .45 Colt that stayed with him for the rest of his life. He also carried a short-barrelled .45 Colt in a shoulder holster that was concealed under his shirt. This weapon was to get him out of trouble on a number of occasions.

Jeff Milton spent the next four years patrolling the sprawling state of Texas enforcing the law in the tented towns that followed the South Pacific railroad as new track was laid across the desert and wastelands into El Paso. These tented towns were full of gamblers, saloons and prostitutes waiting to service and relieve the railroad construction gangs of their hard-earned money. In one incident in Mitchell County an angry, violent cowboy pulled his gun and fired on Jeff Milton and two other Rangers as they tried to arrest him. Jeff Milton and the two other Rangers reacted immediately, returning fire and shooting the man dead. The three Rangers were arrested and put on trial for murder. Threats of lynching were hurled at the three men from cowboys from the dead man's ranch and other ranches. During the preliminary trial, which was carried out in a tense, hostile atmosphere, the three men were guarded by fellow Texas Rangers, each of whom was wearing two guns, one close to the hand of each of the three accused. The would-be lynching parties became aware of this and reduced their threats to mutterings in the local saloons. It took almost three years of legal wrangling before Jeff Milton and his fellow Rangers were acquitted, but in the meantime they continued to carry out their duties as Rangers.

After four years of serving with the Texas Rangers, Jeff Milton moved to New Mexico and took up the position of Deputy US Marshal. He worked briefly with Commodore Perry Owens in the mountain settlement of St John's, Arizona. Perry Owens had a reputation for shooting first and asking questions later, and because of this the partnership didn't last long, as Owens's methods didn't sit too well with Jeff Milton, who was always straight and above board. In early 1877, the collector of customs, Joseph Magoffin of El Paso, recruited him. His new role was to ride alone with a packhorse from Nogales across the desert wastes clear to the Gulf of California. His job was to try and prevent smuggling – one man covering hundreds of miles. The task was an onerous one because at the time just 11 men patrolled the almost waterless stretch from El Paso to the Gulf of California. The dangers they faced were numerous, especially when confronting smugglers and trying to collect customs duty. Jeff Milton, however, had made friends with a number of Papago Indians who helped him more than once to survive in the desert and apprehend some of the more dangerous smugglers. In 1889 a change in the government caused the entire customs service to be brought to an end.

To make ends meet Jeff Milton took up the job of a train conductor on the Southern Pacific railway between El Paso and Mexico City. This route was known to be a bit rowdy, usually due to too much alcohol, but when they found out who the conductor was, (Jeff Milton's reputation having gone before him), things became much quieter, especially when they saw his pistol tucked into his waistband. However one incident caused him to give up the job, and that was when he was alleged to have thrown a drunken Mexican passenger off the train. The man later

Colonel Abner Tibbetts with five of his mounted custom officers.

died of his injuries, and realising that he was not likely to get a fair trial in Mexico, Jeff Milton disguised himself as Mexican and quietly slipped back into the United States.

Two years later he moved to take up the post of deputy sheriff in Cochise County, Arizona, working under Sheriff John Slaughter. The two men became a formidable team and during their time together were involved in a number of successful manhunts and shoot-outs. One of these involved the notorious Jack Taylor gang, which was wanted for train robberies, the murder of a railway engineer and four passengers in Sonora. Jack Taylor specialised in train robberies and had a

John Slaughter.

reputation for being ruthless when confronted by anyone who got in his way. The gang operated mostly in Arizona, New Mexico and Mexico. In 1887 Sheriff Slaughter received a tip-off that four of the gang members, Geronimo Miranda, Manuel Robles, Nieves Deron and Fred Federico were hiding out at the home of a Flora Cardenas. However, word had leaked out that Sheriff Slaughter was on his way with a large posse and by the time they reached the home of Flora Cardenas the members of the gang were long gone. Then word reached them that two of the four men were hiding out at the home of Guadeloupe Robles, brother of Manuel Robles, in Contention City, Arizona. The posse surrounded the house and then stormed it. Sheriff Slaughter killed Guadeloupe Robles when he opened fire as they burst in, while the two other gang members ran behind some rocks at the rear of the house and exchanged gunfire with the posse. Nieves Deron was shot and killed during the gunfight and Manuel Robles was badly wounded but managed to escape through a heavily wooded area.

Later that month word came through that Jack Taylor had been captured in Mexico by Mexican Rurales (Mounted Police), in the act of a robbery in which one of the victims was killed. He was sentenced to life imprisonment in a Mexican gaol. Meanwhile, the two remaining

A group of Mexican Rurales about to go on patrol.

Rurales Mexican Mounted Police about to leave on patrol.

members of the gang, Robles and Miranda, remained at large but were constantly on the run. Robles, who had not fully recovered from his gunshot wounds, was struggling and so the two decided to head for Mexico. As they travelled through the Sierra Madre mountains they were spotted by a Mexican Rurales patrol and during a gunfight both were shot dead. The remaining gang member, Fred Federico, angry at the loss of his fellow gang members and blaming Sheriff John Slaughter, planned an ambush. He unfortunately mistook Deputy Sheriff Cesario Lucero for Sheriff Slaughter and killed him. Within days Sheriff Slaughter and Jeff Milton had tracked him down. He was tried and hanged shortly afterwards.

In 1887, Jeff Milton joined the US Customs Service as a mounted inspector based in El Paso. For the next two years he rode the line from Nogales to the Colorado River, but because his appointment was a federal one he lost his job when a new political party took power. He then took up the post of 'railway spotter' with the Southern Pacific railroad and was wounded after being involved in a number of attempted hold-ups. The job of the 'spotter' was to look out for possible attempts to hold up the train and if necessary defend it.

In 1895 Jeff Milton took up the post of chief of police in El Paso, Texas. At the time there was a serious spate of rustling being carried out by an outlaw by the name of Martin McRose, and Deputy US Marshal George Scarborough was sent to arrest him. George Scarborough joined up with Jeff Milton and, much like Milton's relationship with Sheriff Slaughter, the two of them gained a reputation for their tenacity in hunting down outlaws and became two of the most feared lawmen in Texas. They did however attract some controversy, especially when they were bringing Martin McRose back from Mexico after he had been caught by the Mexicans taking rustled cattle over the border. During the trip back, McRose tried to escape and was shot dead. John Wesley Hardin, who was having an affair with McRose's woman, made a statement that he had paid Milton and Scarborough to kill McRose and make it look like he was trying to escape. Both lawmen were arrested on suspicion of murder, but Hardin later retracted his statement and the two lawmen were released without charge. It is not known why John Wesley Hardin made the statement.

The two lawmen were called into action again in July 1898, when they went after the Walters gang. 'Bronco Bill' Walters's gang was involved in almost anything illegal, from robbery and hold-ups to whisky peddling, and was wanted in several states. When the gang

Jeff Milton with George Scarborough.

entered the territory of Jeff Milton they made their biggest mistake. The two lawmen tracked the gang to their hideout close to Solomonville, Arizona, where they got involved in a shoot-out. In the resulting firestorm 'Bronco Bill' Walters was badly wounded and captured, and another member of the gang was killed. The remaining members of the gang scattered and got away.

Six months later another gang, the Burt Alvord Gang, made its appearance in Fairbank, Arizona. Jeff Milton was aboard a train to Fairbank when the former lawman Burt Alvord and his gang attempted to rob the train. A gunfight ensued between the five members of the gang and Jeff Milton in which one of the gang, 'Three-fingered Jack Dunlop', was killed and another, Bravo Juan Yaos, was wounded, as was Jeff Milton whose left arm was shattered. Just before he passed out, he managed to throw the safe keys into a pile of parcels. The remaining members of the gang searched unsuccessfully for the keys and were about to shoot Jeff Milton when the engineer persuaded them that Milton was already dead. Realising that Jeff Milton was now no threat to them, the three remaining members of the gang took the opportunity to slip away. After hours of surgery and weeks of rehabilitation Jeff Milton was forced to relinquish his position as chief of police as his left arm was now permanently disabled and shorter than his right arm.

Despite his disability, in 1904 Jeff Milton took up the post of Mounted Chinese Inspector with the Bureau of Immigration. Commissioned by President Theodore Roosevelt, Jeff Milton was responsible for enforcing the Chinese Exclusion Act. This position was created when it was discovered that hundreds of Chinese were being smuggled into the USA from Mexico. After 20 years of this he transferred to the US Immigration Service at the age of 62, and for the next eight years patrolled the border with Mexico. Then, at the age of 70, he reluctantly retired when

Burt Alvord, leader of the Alvord gang.

the Economy Act of 1932 came into being and he was forced out.

Jeff Milton remains known as 'the first Border Patrolman'. He moved to Tucson, where his old comrades of the Border Patrol surreptitiously watched over him, until he died on 7 May 1947.

Chapter 28

Captain Harry Love

Captain Harry Love was born in Vermont in around 1820, although the actual date is not known. In fact very little is known about him until the 1850 Californian Gold Rush days. He was a sailor for a short period before ending up in Texas, where, it is claimed, he joined the Texas Rangers. With the advent of the war with Mexico he served, alongside many other Rangers, with the US Army in the Mexican–American War of 1846–48. After the war he drifted west, finding work as an army scout and express rider.

Captain Harry Love, leader of the California Rangers, the first law enforcement organisation in California.

In 1850 the discovery of gold in California sparked the gold rush and Harry Love, like countless others, went to make his fortune, but with no luck. Desperate for work, he became a deputy sheriff of Santa Barbara, California, while still looking for gold. After two years of trying to keep law and order and fruitless mining, he became a bounty hunter. This came about after the family of Allen Ruddle, who was robbed and murdered by three men while driving a wagon to Stockton, had put up a large reward for their capture. Harry Love and an unknown partner tracked the three wanted men to the Rancho San Luis Gonzaga, situated at the foot of Pacheco Pass. On finding them gone when they arrived, they followed one of the three men, Pedro Gonzalez, to Buaenaventura in Santa Barbara County, where they arrested him. Love discovered that Pedro Gonzalez was a member of the notorious Joaquin Murrieta's gang, whom Love suspected was probably behind the robbery and murder of Allen Ruddle. During the trip back to Los Angeles the three men stopped at Cuesta del Conejo for a rest. Gonzalez attempted to escape and was shot dead by Harry Love. The trail of the other members of the gang had gone cold, but Harry Love's reputation had been greatly enhanced by the capture of one of the three members of the gang. On 11 May 1853 the governor of California, John Bigler, named Harry Love as the commander of the newly created California Rangers, tasked with the capture or killing of the 'Five Joaquins Gang', which was known to be responsible for over 20 murders, a large number of robberies and the theft of a number of horses from the goldfields of California.

For the next three months Captain Harry Love and 20 of his Rangers combed the state, searching for the whereabouts of the gang, but they drew a blank. The gang appeared to have vanished. However, as they were searching for the Joaquin Gang they managed to capture a number of other wanted men, albeit not for the most serious of offences. Having no luck tracing the gang, Harry Love and his men decided to widen the search, starting on the far side of the Diablo Range close to San Juan Bautista. Then the Rangers received a tip-off that Joaquin Murrieta's brother-in-law, Jesus Feliz, lived close by. Harry Love promptly arrested him on suspicion of being a member of the Joaquin Murrieta Gang. Jesus Feliz protested his innocence, so Harry Love promised him that he would be set free if he would lead them to the hideout of the Joaquin Murrieta Gang.

After writing a letter to the governor explaining what had happened and what he proposed to do, Captain Harry Love and his Rangers, accompanied by Jesus Feliz, rode southwards towards the Salinas Valley. This was a deliberate ploy in an effort to deceive any informers working for the Joaquin Murrieta gang of their intentions. That same night the group backtracked and headed south-eastward along the San Benito valley and then into the Diablo Range to the Rancho de Los Aguilas. They then followed the trail to La Vereda del Monte, which brought them to a point overlooking the Arroya de Cantua, which was the hideout of the Joaquin Murrieta Gang. The Rangers saw hundreds of horses, some obviously stolen, others unbroken wild ones, being handled by over 80 men. Some of the horses were being rebranded, others broken, but all were being prepared for sale at Sonora. After being given assurance that this was where Joaquin Murrieta and his

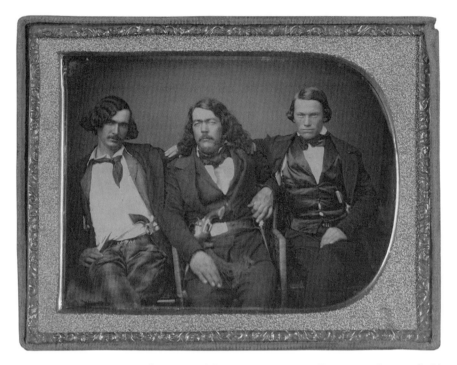

Captain Harry Love with two California Rangers, William Henderson (left) and an unknown Ranger.

gang were, Harry Love sent Jesus Feliz away and with some of his Rangers rode down into the valley.

After convincing members of the gang that they wanted to buy some of the horses, they picked out some of the obviously branded stolen ones, saying that they were returning to San Juan and that they would be back to collect them. The following day the Rangers returned to observe the gang, only to find the place deserted. The Rangers waited until the early hours of the following morning before heading down the valley to the south-east.

After some days of travelling the Rangers encountered a small group of seven Mexicans just south of the Arroyo de Cantua in Mariposa County. What happened next became a controversial incident that was argued about for many years. The Rangers version was that a confrontation occurred which resulted in a gunfight between the two groups. Four of the Mexicans were killed, two were wounded and captured, and the remaining three escaped. It was also claimed that two of the Mexicans killed were Joaquin Murrieta and Emanuel Garcia (aka 'Three Fingered Jack'). To prove that they were the wanted men, and enabling them

Above left: Joaquim Murrieta.

Above right: Said to be the head of Joaquim Murrieta.

to claim the reward, they cut off the heads of both men as well as the three-fingered hand of Garcia. An express rider took them to Fort Miller where the gruesome remains were pickled in brandy in an effort to preserve them. Emanuel Garcia's head had a bullet shot through it and decayed rapidly in the summer heat and was subsequently buried in Fort Miller. The head of Joaquin Murrieta and the hand of Garcia were put on display for a while before being taken around California where they could be viewed at the cost of $1.

A large number of people testified that the head was that of Joaquin Murrieta, including a priest. This enabled the Rangers to collect the reward money. A little while later a young woman, who claimed to be Murrieta's sister, said that it was not the head of her brother because it did not have a scar on the face. There were also a number of claims of sightings of Joaquin Murrieta around California, but none could be substantiated. It was also rumoured that the Rangers had actually killed some innocent Mexican cowboys and made up the story of the gunfight in order to collect the reward. These rumours were to follow Captain Harry Love for the remainder of his life. The head and the hand were lost during the San Francisco Earthquake in 1906.

The capture and death of Joaquin Murrieta caused the California Rangers to be disbanded. Harry Love bought himself a large piece of land near Boulder Creek in Santa Cruz County and settled down after marrying Mary Bennett, a widow who lived in a nearby ranch. This did not work out for Harry Love and his wife: it was a tempestuous relationship and Mary Bennett moved back to her own ranch. She later sued for divorce but lost. Harry Love lost his property due to an accumulation of things, including a fire, floods and squatters who completely destroyed the house. His estranged wife had a small house built on her property where Harry Love could live, but she would not allow him into the main house. So fearful of him was she, that she hired a bodyguard and, after one confrontation in which Harry Love attempted to shoot the bodyguard, he himself was wounded in the exchange of gunfire.

In an attempt to save his life doctors amputated his arm, but he died from an infection. He was buried in an unmarked grave, but years later a headstone was put up in Mission City Memorial Park in Santa Clara, which read:

HERE LIES CAPTAIN HARRY LOVE, WHO WITH A TROOP OF TWENTY OTHERS, ON JULY 25, 1853 ALLEGEDLY KILLED BANDITS JOAQUIN MURRIETTA AND THREE FINGERED JACK NEAR ARROYO DE CANTUA, FRESNO COUNTY, CALIFORNIA.

BORN IN VERMONT, LOVE FIRST VISITED ALTA CALIFORNIA AS A SEAMAN IN 1839. HE SERVED IN THE MEXICAN WAR OF 1846 AND LATER AS AN ARMY EXPRESS RIDER AND EXPLORER OF THE RIO GRANDE. LOVE ARRIVED IN SAN FRANCISCO IN DECEMBER OF 1850 AND TOOK RESIDENCE IN MARIPOSA COUNTY. HE WAS COMMISSIONED AS CAPTAIN OF THE CALIFORNIA RANGERS ON MAY 28, 1853 AND IN THE FOLLOWING YEAR MARRIED MARY McSWAIN BENNETT OF SANTA CLARA.

CAPTAIN HARRY LOVE DIED IN THE MISSION CITY ON JUNE 29, 1868 FROM A WOUND RECEIVED IN A GUNFIGHT WITH AN EMPLOYEE OF HIS THEN ESTRANGED WIFE.

Chapter 29

Dan Tucker

Dan Tucker was born in Canada in 1849. Little is known about him until 1875 when he appeared in Grant County, New Mexico. The county sheriff, Harvey Whitehill, had heard rumours about his involvement in a shooting in Colorado, but took an instant liking to the quiet, well-spoken young man and took him on as a deputy sheriff.

Dan Tucker's first encounter with lawbreakers as a deputy came when two Mexicans got into a fight in the local dance hall in Silver City. One of the Mexicans stabbed and wounded the other man, then ran out of the dance hall just as Dan Tucker, who had been summoned by the owner of the dance hall, arrived. Dan Tucker quickly drew his pistol and shot the man dead. A couple of months later he was called again to deal with a drunken Mexican, who was standing in the middle of the street throwing rocks at people passing by. A number of people were hurt and when told to stop by Dan Tucker, the man threw a rock at him. Dan Tucker drew his pistol and shot the man dead. Both these incidents were deemed to have been carried out lawfully and no charges were brought against him.

The local people were impressed by Dan Tucker and the following year, 1877, appointed him the gaoler for Silver City, New Mexico. This appointment was short-lived, as a couple of months later the El Paso Salt War erupted. Dan Tucker, with 30 men from Silver City, was sent to assist Sheriff Charles Kerber and some members of the Texas Rangers and the US Army in a fight with Mexican bandits at San Elizario. The 'war' started over a dispute over title to the salt deposits at the base of the Guadalupe Mountains. The local San Elizario Texas Mexican community had been collecting the salt deposits for free for years, but a large company had always claimed title over the salt. The dispute escalated into violence and, after a number of killings, the law took control and the Mexican community was forced to pay for the salt they had been collecting for free for years.

The following year, 1878, Dan Tucker was appointed as the first town marshal of Silver City, but also continued to serve as a deputy sheriff of Grant County, which gave him greater powers in a wider area to enforce the law. One of his first acts as town marshal was to ban the firing of guns in the street, which some of the local cowboys were prone to do on pay nights. Over the next few months Dan Tucker stamped his authority on the town and a couple of incidents exemplified this. The first was when he caught a thief trying to escape and shot him dead, and the second was a gunfight with three horse thieves inside the Silver City Saloon, when he killed two of the thieves and wounded the third. In November Tucker himself was shot and wounded when he tried to arrest a cowboy by the name of Caprio Rodriguez. The man resisted and a gunfight ensued, which in the end left Dan Tucker wounded and Rodriguez dead in the street. Later that month Dan Tucker resigned as city marshal, but was reappointed in May the following year. It was said that his attitude to law and order was to shoot first and ask questions afterwards.

Silver City was now a relatively quiet town, with the law strictly in control. Then, in 1880, Dan Tucker was asked to go to the mining town of Shakespeare, New Mexico, after two thieves had broken into a prospector's cabin and stolen several items. Dan Tucker set off on the

Part of the mining town of Shakespeare.

trail of the two men and returned a couple of days later with all of the stolen property, plus two saddles and weapons. When asked about the thieves he replied that he had found them on a ranch and had killed them both when they refused to give themselves up. The ranch owner agreed to bury the men on his property. In another incident he was called to deal with a domestic dispute when a man had almost beaten his wife to death. On entering the house the man had attacked Dan Tucker, but following a short scuffle he was shot dead. The following year Dan Tucker was appointed the city marshal for Shakespeare and almost immediately stamped his authority on the town by shooting dead a wanted cattle rustler, Jake Bond. One month later he shot dead a cowboy who rode his horse into the dining room of the local hotel. A week after that he arrested two outlaws, Sandy King and 'Russian Bill' Tattenbaum. The town's Vigilante Committee later unlawfully

Grant House, Shakespeare, New Mexico.

hanged the two outlaws inside a building called the Grant House.

Such was his reputation of, 'shoot first, ask questions afterwards', that in November 1881 Dan Tucker was sent by the governor of New Mexico to the town of Deming to restore law and order as a gang of outlaws was terrifying the townspeople. The moment he arrived Dan Tucker started to patrol the streets with a shotgun in the crook of his arm and a Colt six-gun in a holster on his hip. Within three days, three of the outlaws were dead and two more seriously wounded, and

Left: Grant House, Shakespeare, New Mexico, showing hanging room.

Below: The hanging room in Grant House.

law and order had been restored. In 1881 he had arrested 13 members of a gang and killed at least four more, bringing his brand of law and order to the towns of Shakespeare, Deming and Silver City. He was without doubt one of the most feared lawmen in New Mexico, and it was said that Wyatt Earp and Doc Holiday, who had had to leave Tombstone in a hurry after the OK Corral incident, avoided Deming by going on horseback around the town rather than risk going through it on the train because of arrest warrants having been issued against them. After these incidents Tucker became known as Dangerous Dan.

In August 1882, while a deputy town marshal in the mining town of Paschal, New Mexico, Tucker became involved in a controversial shooting incident concerning one of the other deputies. It started when Deputy James Burns had been drinking over a two-day period and staggered into the Centennial Saloon waving his pistol about and threatening customers with it. The town marshal, Claudius Moore, and another deputy tried to disarm Burns, but he refused, saying that he was an officer of the law and entitled to carry a gun. Later that afternoon, still drunk, he started to wave his gun about again. In the meantime Dan Tucker had entered the saloon and when the town marshal tried again to disarm him Burns refused, pointing his gun at him. Next moment there was a shot, and although no one was hit, Dan Tucker pulled his Colt from its holster and fired, hitting Burns in the chest. One second later the town marshal also fired, killing Burns. There was a hostile reaction to the shooting because Burns was popular among the miners who frequented the saloons, but an enquiry into the shooting cleared both lawmen. However, Claudius Moore was dismissed as town marshal, but Dan Tucker remained for a short while before he returned to Deming.

On 14 December 1882, Dan Tucker, now back as town marshal of Deming, was called upon to investigate a complaint from someone in the local brothel. On entering the building he was fired on and hit in the shoulder, but pulling out his own gun he returned fire, killing both the Mexican gunman and the prostitute who had lured him in with the false complaint.

In October 1883 Tucker was appointed Deputy US Marshal for New Mexico and within the month was engaged in a successful battle, alongside another deputy, with renegade Apache warriors just outside Deming. Dan Tucker continued to enforce the law over the next few years, but in 1888 he suddenly resigned his appointment and went to California. This was the last time he was ever seen, although it was said that he visited Grant County in May 1892, but that was never confirmed.

191

Centennial Saloon, New Mexico, owned by Dangerous Dan Tucker.

Dan Tucker has since been recognised as one of the most feared lawmen in the Old West, as well as being one of the most underestimated and dangerous gunmen. It is thought that he killed more than 17 criminals during his career and arrested dozens more. As one historian put it:

'Dan Tucker was a better lawman, and more dangerous, than such redoubtable characters as Wyatt Earp and Wild Bill Hickock'.

Chapter 30

Timothy Isaiah Courtright

'Longhair Jim' or 'Big Jim' Courtright

Tim Courtright was born in Sangamon County, Illinois, in the spring of 1848, the son of Daniel Courtright. He had four older sisters and one younger brother. From a very early age he was interested in guns and is said to have practised shooting frequently. At the start of the American Civil War he lied about his age and enlisted in the Union Army and served under General John A. Logan. During one battle he took a bullet aimed at the general and earned Logan's admiration. At the end of the Civil War Tim Courtright travelled around doing odd jobs. In 1875 he met and married Sarah Weeks and taught her how to shoot. They held shooting exhibitions for which they charged admission, and later performed as part of Buffalo Bill's *Wild West Show*.

In 1876 Tim Courtright and his wife arrived in Fort Worth, Texas. After settling down he ran to be the first elected town marshal against four other men, winning by three votes. He liked to be noticed and wore his hair long and carried two revolvers on his hips, with their butts facing forward. He also became known for using his badge to extract protection money from town business owners.

As town marshal, Courtright was in charge of keeping the peace in the notorious 'Hell's Half Acre' (the town's red light district). Before his appointment Fort Worth had acquired a reputation as a very dangerous place, with

Sheriff Jim Courtright.

fights between unruly drunks and lawmen being commonplace. With the appointment of Tim Courtright as town marshal, few people dared to cross him, and it is known that he killed several who did. On 25 August 1877, Deputy Marshal Columbus Fitzgerald was shot and killed while attempting to break up a street fight. Tim Courtright immediately went looking for the man who had killed him, found the culprit and shot and killed him that same night. During his time as town marshal, it is reported that he killed at least four other men during altercations and shoot-outs. Within his first term of office he successfully reduced Fort Worth's murder rate by more than half, but he also acquired a reputation of being fast with a gun, and spontaneous in his reaction to trouble. It is also thought that he murdered several unwilling business owners who would not pay into his protection racket. Most met his demands in order to avoid becoming the target of his anger and gun. Some who declined were killed, and those who survived usually made the payments demanded.

Tim Courtright served as Fort Worth's marshal until 1879, when he lost his third election. Leaving his family behind in Fort Worth, he moved to New Mexico and became the town marshal of Lake Valley, California, then later he became a hired guard for a mining operation. Sometime later, while working as a ranch foreman, he and his friend Jim McIntire shot and killed two squatters who had refused to leave the ranch.

The incident concerned his former Civil War commander, General John Logan, who wanted to buy the American Valley Cattle Company in New Mexico. The company owned a vast tract of land some 66 by 72 miles wide, and had complained about rustlers that were stealing cattle from the vast herds that were grazing on the land. US Marshal A. Morisson empowered Tim Courtright and Jim McIntire to hunt down the rustlers. The current owner of the company, John Casey, together with his partners William Moore and Henry Atkison, were not that interested in selling as they had bigger plans for the company that included purchasing an additional 3,400 acres with water rights. If successful that would allow them to take control of 3,000,000 acres of grazing land. Standing in their way were the owners of a small ranch, Alexis Grossetete and Robert Elsinger, who had claimed their land under the pre-emption rights that guaranteed settlers the right to file a patent on unsurveyed land. They made it quite clear that they were not prepared to leave. John Casey regarded them as squatters and was determined to get them off what he deemed to be his land.

One of the company's partners, William Moore, had in the past worked for the LX Ranch in the Texas Panhandle as the manager of their large herd. The owners of the ranch later discovered that he was quietly rustling cattle for himself and building a herd of his own on his ranch at Adobe Wells. He was dismissed immediately, but within weeks had sold his ranch for $75,000, using $25,000 to buy a one-third interest in the American Valley Cattle Company.

Tim Courtright and Jim McIntire initially thought they were on the trail of rustlers, but then were told that they were looking for a former employee of John Casey's named Dave Gilmore, believed to be in a cabin near Socorro, New Mexico. The posse of six men, led by William Moore, arrived at a line cabin eight miles from the ranch belonging to Grossetete and Elsinger. After staying the night at the cabin, the following morning they were told that the reason they were there was to get rid of the 'squatters'. Moore told the posse that they were to take the men out of the house and kill them and that all six of them would fire into the bodies, making them equally guilty of the killings. The early morning raid surprised the men and they were taken to a narrow ravine and killed.

The foreman of John Casey's ranch, Daniel McAllister, on hearing of the killings, told the authorities, who immediately issued warrants for the arrest of William Moore and the members of the posse. Ironically, Tim Courtright and Jim McIntire, who were lawmen, were tasked with bringing in the men, but at the grand jury arraignment it was learned that both Courtright and McIntire had been part of the posse. William Moore had escaped, and before they too could be arrested, Courtright and McIntire headed for Mexico on horseback. They went to El Paso, Texas, where they knew a number of former Texas Rangers and remained there until everything had cooled down. Both men later returned to Fort Worth and, after a number of legal arguments in which they said they were acting lawfully as lawmen, they successfully fought off extradition to New Mexico. The two men then had their families join them. In New Mexico two other members of the posse had been tried in respect of the murders and both were acquitted.

Tim Courtright's reputation was now firmly established and he continued running his protection racket in Fort Worth, despite being warned by the town marshal. Things came to a head when Luke Short arrived to manage the White Elephant Saloon and gambling house. Luke Short was a renowned gunfighter and gambler with a reputation for not backing down to anyone. Courtright approached Short and offered him protection for the White Elephant for a fee, but Short made it clear that he did not want protection and was more than capable of dealing with any trouble himself.

Courtright was furious and realised that to save face he had to deal with Luke Short. On 8 February 1887, he stood outside the White Elephant and called Luke Short out. A friend of Courtright's, Jake Johnson, tried to reason with him and momentarily calmed things down. But then Luke Short appeared and the two men walked down the street and stopped in front of Ella Blackwell's bar and brothel and faced each other, standing three to four feet apart. Without saying a word, they drew their pistols. A number of different accounts of what happened all came to the same conclusion: Luke Short was faster on the draw than Tim Courtright. One account said that Luke Short's first shot hit Courtright's gun and took off his thumb, while another, by Bat Masterson, said that Luke Short put five bullets into Courtright before he hit the ground. The result was the same – Tim Courtright was dead. There is no doubt that a number of business owners weren't sorry to see the end of him and his protection racket.

Luke Short was arrested and tried for the shooting, but was acquitted on the grounds of self-defence as it was deemed that Tim Courtright had started it by calling Luke Short out for a confrontation. Despite being on both sides of the law at different times, like many other lawmen at the time, Tim Courtright did manage to keep law and order in a number of places.

Chapter 31

Deputy Sheriff John Selman

John Henry Selman was one of those lawmen who lived on both sides of the law. Born in Madison County, Arkansas, in 1843, in 1858 the family moved to Grayson County, Texas. Shortly after his father's death. John Selman joined the 22nd Texas Cavalry and fought during the American Civil War. Close to the end of the war he deserted and returned home, where he met Edna Degraffenreid. They were married on 17 August 1865 and settled down in Grayson County. During the next 10 years almost nothing is known about John Selman other than that he had four children. In 1877 the family moved to Fort Griffin in Shackelford County, Texas, where he took up the post of Deputy Inspector for Hides working under inspector and ex-Shackelford County Sheriff John Larn. The two men worked well together and were involved in a number of incidents with outlaws and rustlers in which a number of them were killed.

In 1878 John Selman learned that John Larn had been arrested after six hides were found hidden behind Larn's house that had brands on them belonging to a couple of ranchers. When sheriff of Shackelford County, John Larn had been involved with vigilantes who went after rustlers and those who were caught were lynched without trial. John Larn went on the run, but was caught by the local sheriff and put in gaol in Albany, Texas. The sheriff, concerned

John Henry Selman when a constable in El Paso, Texas.

The gaol and Fort Griffin.

that some of Larn's friends would try and break him out, chained him to the floor of his cell. Vigilantes broke in to the gaol, and because they could not get him out to hang, shot him dead in his cell. John Selman found himself implicated in the discovery of the hides because of his close association with John Larn and also went on the run. He also thought that he was still wanted for desertion from the Confederate Army and so he headed for Mexico. At the end of the war and after the dissolution of the Confederacy all charges of desertion were deemed to be null and void, and after discovering this John Selman returned to the United States to find that his wife had died. His wife's niece took in his four children and John Selman went to live in Lincoln County, New Mexico. He arrived at the time of the start of the Lincoln County Wars and quickly got involved by organising a band of men who became known as 'Selman's Scouts', or among locals 'The Rustlers'. Throughout the 'war' they were accused of murder, rape and rustling, although no charges were ever brought against them.

John Selman kept a tight grip on his men and when one of them, Roscoe Bryant, was involved in something outside of the activities of

Selman's Scouts, he was summarily dealt with and his body dumped near Seven Rivers, New Mexico. Besides the Lincoln County Wars, there were a number of other incidents including the HooDoo War, the El Paso Salt War, the Sutton-Taylor Feud and the Lee-Peacock Feud. Nearly all these wars and feuds were continuances of the Civil War and the reconstruction of the south. Arguments about land ownership were rife, and legally sorting out the rights and wrongs of these disputes was almost impossible. John Selman was involved in many ways either through family or just simply personal involvement. In between, Mexican bandits would take advantage of the hostilities, cross the border and rustle cattle from the various ranches leaving the ranchers accusing each other. Selman's Scouts were also very active during this period, but by 1880 things had quietened down and the various ranchers were finally able to drive John Selman and his band out of Lincoln County. The band moved to Jeff Davis County and began their operation there, but it wasn't long before the law caught up with them and the capture of John Selman by Texas Ranger Joe McKidrict brought the reign of terror to an end. He was taken to Shackelford County to stand trial, but managed to escape and fled to Chihuahua, Mexico, taking his two youngest boys with him. The remaining two children stayed behind in Brown County, Texas, and were never to see their father again.

For the next eight years, John Selman and his two young sons led a very quiet life, Selman all the time protesting his innocence. Then, in 1888, when all the charges against him were dropped due to lack of evidence or witnesses, he and his sons returned to the United States.

John Selman and his sons moved to El Paso, Texas, where he had a variety of jobs. Three years later he married Romula Granadine and took up the position of town constable. A year later he was involved in an incident with a former Texas Ranger by the name of Bass Outlaw. Outlaw had recently been dismissed from the Rangers because of his excessive drinking and threats he had made against a judge who had admonished him for his behaviour. John Selman had been on duty when he came across a drunken Bass Outlaw and told him to go home and sleep it off. Bass Outlaw refused and headed towards a nearby brothel called 'Tillie Howard', a regular haunt of his. On entering the premises, Outlaw created a disturbance, which drew the attention of Texas Ranger Joe McKidrict. Shots were fired and McKidrict fell down fatally wounded. On hearing the gunshots John Selman went inside and was shot twice in the thigh, but managed to return fire and kill Bass Outlaw. The killing of Bass Outlaw by John Selman was considered to be justified as he had fired in self-defence.

199

Soon after the incident John Selman Jnr joined the El Paso police force working with his father. Then, on 19 August 1895, John Selman Jnr arrested a lady by the name of Beluah M'rose who was drunk and brandishing a gun in the air and uttering threats. The lady in question was the mistress of John Wesley Hardin, who confronted John Jnr and the two had a violent verbal argument in the street. The row escalated when Hardin pulled out his gun and pistol-whipped the young constable and threatened his life. On hearing of the incident John Selman Snr approached Hardin and the two exchanged strong and angry words. That evening Hardin was in the Acme saloon gambling when John Selman entered with a pistol in his hand. He walked up behind John Wesley Hardin, placed the pistol to the back of his head and pulled the trigger. As Hardin hit the floor Selman fired another three shots into his chest and Hardin died instantly. Selman claimed that Hardin had seen him enter in a mirror and was in the process of drawing his gun when Selman shot him in self-defence. After a trial and a hung jury, a retrial was ordered.

Six months later, John Selman was playing cards with Deputy US Marshal George Scarborough when an argument broke out between them. It was initially said that Scarborough was a close friend of Bass

Outlaw and that he was angry about Selman shooting him. This was probably not true as Selman and Scarborough were quite close friends and Outlaw was a disgraced Texas Ranger not liked by fellow Rangers. It transpired that the young John Selman had got himself romantically involved with a Mexican girl and had eloped. Her father, a diplomat, went looking for them and when found young Selman was imprisoned in Juarez, Mexico. When John Selman discovered this he approached George Scarborough to help him get his son out of gaol, to which he agreed. The pair of them had been drinking for most of the evening and after the discussion John Selman invited George Scarborough to have a drink with him. George Scarborough declined, feeling that he had had enough to drink. For some unknown reason John Selman

Sheriff John Selman, killer of John Wesley Hardin.

took offence, drew his gun and fired, but missed. Scarborough drew his gun and shot John Selman in self-defence. Selman died a few hours later from the wound.

George Scarborough was arrested and charged with the murder of John Selman when it was discovered that John Selman's gun was not at the scene of the shooting. Just before his trial was to begin, a man named Cole Belmont, a known thief, was arrested and on being searched was found to have John Selman's gun in his possession. He admitted to having seen the shooting and being first on the scene. On seeing the gun lying on the floor he had picked it up before anyone else arrived. George Scarborough was released without charge.

John Selman was buried in the local El Paso churchyard. What happened to his son, John Selman Jnr, is not known.

Chapter 32

Charles Bassett

Charles E. Bassett was born on 30 October 1847 in New Bedford, Massachusetts, the fourth of six children born to Benjamin and Julia Bassett. Charlie was in his late teens when his parents separated, and he elected to live with his father in Philadelphia. At the age of 18, on 14 February 1865, he enlisted in the Union Army, signing on for one year. He received a $100 signing-on fee and was assigned to the 213th Pennsylvania Infantry Volunteer Regiment in Washington, DC as a private. His enlistment was terminated less than a year later, mainly because of the army having to cut back on the number of troops they needed after General Lee had surrendered the Confederate Army in April.

Sheriff Charles Bassett, city marshal of Dodge City.

For the next eight years or so Charles Bassett drifted around the West doing various jobs, including buffalo hunter, bartender and miner. In 1872 he ended up in Dodge City, Kansas, where he met a man by the name of Alfred J. Peacock, and together they opened the Long Branch Saloon. One year later they sold the saloon and over the next few years it changed hands several times until, in 1882, it was purchased by a gambler by the name of Luke Short. Short was to feature largely in Bassett's life soon after.

On 5 June 1873, the position of sheriff for Ford County, Kansas, was advertised

Inside the Long Branch Saloon, Dodge City.

Long Branch Saloon, Dodge City.

and Charles Bassett was appointed their first sheriff. His office was in Dodge City, and with the help of deputies Bat Masterson and Jon Webb, maintained law and order. So popular did he become, that he was re-elected twice. In his last year as sheriff, he and his deputies went after the notorious Sam Bass gang that had robbed a Union Pacific train of $60,000 at Big Springs, Nebraska, and was reported to have been seen in Kansas. Despite days in the saddle the posse had to give up and return to Dodge City, unsuccessful in their pursuit of the train robbers.

When re-election time came up Charles Bassett was not allowed to put his name forward because under Kansas law, no one could seek a third successive term as sheriff of Ford County. The obvious choice was Bassett's deputy, Bat Masterson, and on 6 November 1877, Masterson was elected sheriff of Ford County. His first act was to appoint Charles Bassett as his under-sheriff, although Bassett was also serving as deputy city marshal under Bat Masterson's brother, City Marshal Ed Masterson.

Dodge City seemed to attract train robbers, as on 27 January 1878 Dave Rudabaugh and four of his gang attempted to hold up a train at the small town of Kinsley, Kansas. A posse from Dodge City, led by Bat Masterson, trailed the robbers and captured two of them, Dave Rudabaugh and Edgar West, after a brief fight. A couple of weeks later two more suspected train robbers were arrested by Bat Masterson and Charles Bassett, right in the centre of Dodge City itself. The year had started well for the law, but then tragedy struck on 9 April 1878 when City Marshal Ed Masterson was shot and killed by a Texan cowboy called Jack Wagner. At the beginning of the month Ed Masterson had introduced a law banning the carrying of guns within the city limits. Ed had been called to a nearby saloon where a drunken cowboy was waving a gun about. In an attempt to disarm the man Ed Masterson was shot in his right side and although badly wounded staggered out into the street, followed by Wagner. His brother Bat, on hearing the shot, ran outside just in time to see his brother stagger into the street and fall to the ground. He immediately opened fire with his handgun, shooting Jack Wagner in the stomach, and then turned his gun on Alfred Walker, who was Wagner's boss, and shot him in the arm and in the lung. Ed Masterson died 30 minutes later, while Jack Wagner died the following morning. There is some dispute about Alfred Walker: one report said that he died in Dodge City, while another said he was taken back to Texas and made a full recovery.

After the funeral of Ed Masterson, Charles Bassett was immediately appointed city marshal and the following month he in turn appointed Wyatt Earp as his deputy. Things quietened down for a while, with the town still stunned at the death of their city marshal. Then, on 29 July, the son of wealthy cattle baron Mifflin Kenedy, James 'Spike' Kenedy, tried to shoot Mayor James Kelley. Fortunately he was prevented from doing so by Charles Bassett, who happened to be watching him at the time. After appearing in court, Kenedy was fined and ordered to pay costs. He left town immediately after. The reason for the attack on the mayor is not known, but it is believed that Spike Kenedy held some sort of grudge. Three weeks later he was back in court after being arrested

Dodge City Peace Commission. Top row, left to right: Will Harris, Luke Short, Bat Masterson, W.F. Petillon. Front row: Charlie Bassett, Wyatt Earp, Frank McLean, Neil Brown.

for being drunk and disorderly. He was once again fined and ordered to pay the costs, but this time Charles Bassett told him to leave Dodge and not to come back.

Two months later, in the early hours of the morning, Kenedy crept back into Dodge City and fired two shots through the door of a shack that belonged to Mayor Kelley. The bullets were aimed deliberately at the bed area, but Mayor Kelley was not there and the bed was occupied by a 34-year-old woman by the name of Dora Hard, who was lodging there at the time. She was killed instantly. Immediately a posse was organised and that afternoon City Marshal Charles Bassett, deputy marshals Wyatt Earp and Bill Tilgham, Sheriff Bat Masterson and Deputy Sheriff William Duffey left to catch up with Kenedy. After riding hard for the rest of the day and the following morning, the posse caught up with Kenedy, who on seeing the posse, tried to make a run for it. Members of the posse opened fire, killing his horse and shattering his left arm. Kenedy was arrested for the murder of Dora Hard and returned to Dodge City to stand trial. Three weeks later charges against Kenedy were dropped due to a lack of any incriminating evidence, despite everyone knowing that Kenedy held a long-time grudge against Mayor Kelley. One can only assume that having a very rich father can sometimes tilt the scales of justice.

On 4 November 1879 Charles Bassett resigned as city marshal and was replaced by James Masterson, brother of Bat. Dodge City was now a relatively quiet place compared to what it was when Bassett first arrived, so maybe he thought it was time to move on. Charles Bassett joined up with another ex-lawman, 'Mysterious' Dave Mather, and two other friends and headed for Colorado. For the next two years the four men unsuccessfully panned for gold then decided to call it a day. Bassett and Mather drifted back into Texas and Mexico and for the next couple of years did various jobs. He and Mather split up, Mather staying in Texas while Bassett headed back to Dodge City. He stayed for about a month before being offered a job to manage the Webster and Hughes Marble Hall Saloon in Kansas City, Missouri.

Within a couple of months of Bassett being in Kansas City the Dodge City War erupted. This had come about after Luke Short, who had taken over the Long Branch Saloon in Dodge City, had been 'run out' of the town. He had then headed straight for Kansas City where he knew his friend Charles Bassett was living. Charles Bassett still had some influence in Dodge City and he returned with Luke Short and helped him get re-established. It did help somewhat to have Bat Masterson, Wyatt Earp and a number of other townspeople behind you when you tried to broker out a deal. The bloodless Dodge City War ended with a tenuous truce that was maintained by the Dodge City Peace Commission. With a semblance of peace restored, Charles Bassett returned to Kansas City and opened another saloon called the Senate Saloon. Within a couple of years it had folded and Charles Bassett was reduced to working as a bartender. He later moved to Hot Springs, Arkansas, where he died on 5 January 1896 at the age of 48.

Chapter 33

John Slaughter

John Slaughter imposed the law with his six-shooter and sawn-off double-barrelled shotgun and, it is said, cleaned up the Arizona Territory more than any other individual lawman.

Born in 1841 on a southern plantation in the Sabine Parish near the town of Many in western Louisiana, John Slaughter was just three months old when his parents, Benjamin and Minerva Slaughter, moved to Texas to raise cattle. After leaving school he learned to ride and control the herds by the side of Mexican vaqueros who worked for his father, who also taught him how to speak Spanish. At the age of 20 he joined the Texas Rangers and was soon defending settlers against the Comanche Indians who resented the settlers taking over their land.

Although only 5ft 6in tall and of slight build, Slaughter had piercing black eyes and an attitude that gave the impression he was not a man to tangle with. He joined the Confederate Army's Third Frontier Division, Texas State Troops in Burnet County and for the next two years fought against the Union Army. In 1864 he contracted typhoid fever and was sent home to recuperate. When fully recovered he returned to the fighting, gaining a reputation as a fearless soldier.

A well-armed Sheriff John Slaughter of Cochise County.

At the end of the war John Slaughter and his brothers created the Antonio Ranch Company in Atascosa County, Texas. Here they not only raised cattle, but also moved herds to Mexico, California, Kansas and New Mexico and were among the first to drive cattle along the Chisholm Trail. It was while on a cattle drive to California that John Slaughter developed a liking for the game of poker that ultimately turned into a compulsion. It was this compulsion for poker that was to cause him to have his first brush with the law. He was playing a poker game in a saloon in San Antonio, Texas, when he suspected one of the players, a man named Barney Gallagher, was cheating. When Gallagher won a hand that involved a considerable amount of money, John Slaughter challenged him, pulling his gun as he did so. Picking up all the money he had lost, he left the saloon and headed back to his ranch. Gallagher, incensed at being caught cheating and being exposed in front of the other players and in front of customers, followed John Slaughter to his ranch. On arriving he called Slaughter out to face him. The foreman told Gallagher that he would tell him when he saw him and at that moment John Slaughter appeared on horseback in the distance. Gallagher waited until John Slaughter got closer, and seeing that he was not wearing a gun waited a little while longer, not knowing that John Slaughter always carried a gun in a holster attached to his saddle. Seeing Gallagher with a shotgun across his lap and knowing that the man was out to get revenge he quickly pulled his revolver from its holster and, as he did so, Gallagher raised his gun and fired, but missed. John Slaughter immediately fired back, hitting Gallagher in the heart and killing him instantly. The sheriff was called and all agreed that it was a case of self-defence and nothing more was said.

By the end of the 1870s, John Slaughter, who had married Eliza Adeline Harris and had four children with her, decided that Texas was becoming overcrowded. After discussing it with his wife, he decided to look for somewhere else to live and headed for New Mexico. Leaving his wife and two children (the other two had died when very young), he set out. Initially he planned to start a ranch, but then, in the early 1880s, he decided that Arizona offered better prospects and settled down in Charleston after purchasing the San Bernardino Ranch near Douglas on the US/Mexican border. Once established, he sent for his wife and children, only to discover that his wife had died of smallpox and his children were living with relatives.

Just two years after settling down, John Slaughter was elected sheriff of Cochise County, Arizona, during which time he helped track the renegade Apaches led by Geronimo, actually catching him on the San

Bernardino Ranch. He was also responsible for catching the Jack Taylor Gang and bringing them to justice.

The Jack Taylor Gang was a notorious and ruthless bunch of outlaws specialising in train robberies. They were also wanted for the murder of a train engineer and four passengers. John Slaughter, together with his deputy Jeff Milton, went to the home of Flora Cardenas after a tip-off that several members of the gang were hiding out there. By the time the posse arrived they were gone, but the posse managed to track them down to Contention City, Arizona, and the home of Guadeloupe Roubles, brother of Manuel Roubles, one of the gang. John Slaughter stormed the house, shooting dead Guadeloupe Roubles, while two of the gang, Manuel Roubles and Nieves Deron, ran out of the back. One member of the posse shot down Deron as he was running and killed him, Roubles was wounded but managed to get away. Later that month Jack Taylor was captured by Mexican Rurales and sentenced to life imprisonment. Manuel Roubles and Geronimo Miranda, another member of the gang, were shot dead by Mexican Rurales after a gunfight in the Sierra Madre Occidental Mountains. The last member of the gang, Fred Federico, tried to ambush and kill John Slaughter, but shot dead the wrong man. He was captured soon after and hanged.

John Slaughter later married 18-year-old Cora Howell, and although they had no children of their own, they adopted several including 'Apache May', whom John Slaughter found with Geronimo's Apache renegades.

Retiring as a lawman, John Slaughter bought a meat market in Charleston and two butcher shops in Bisbee and became a very successful businessman. John Slaughter died in Douglas, Arizona, in 1922.

Chapter 34

David Fannin

The lengths some of the deputies went to, to arrest wanted men, was staggering, as in the case of Deputy US Marshal David Fannin. He was sent to arrest a Creole Indian by the name of Jason Lebreu, who was wanted for the rape and murder of a young girl by the name of Leona Devere, the daughter of a wealthy farmer. Lebrue had befriended the girl, who went for a walk with him into a meadow. It was there that he attacked and raped her before forcing her face down into creek, drowning her. Fannin tracked Lebreu to a farm in the Chickasaw Nation where he was working as a farmhand. Lebreu was a dangerous individual, wanted in Texas and New Orleans for murder. Fannin, dressed in old work clothes, persuaded the farmer to hire him to help with the spring planting.

Fannin soon found himself working alongside Lebreu and slowly gained his confidence, but was wary of making a move because Lebreu always carried his Winchester rifle across his back. In one quiet moment Lebreu 'confessed' to having killed a man, saying, as if talking to himself, 'I didn't mean to kill him but I had to'. Fannin asked him what he meant, to which Lebreu replied that he had been working for a rancher and had been caught stealing his cattle and there was no way he could go back to Texas as there was a warrant out for his arrest. Lebreu boasted that he had killed over a dozen men and a young girl and never lost a night's sleep over it. Fannin chose his moment carefully and took it the moment Lebreu placed his rifle against the door as he washed. In one movement Fannin snatched up the rifle and pointed it at the wanted man. After telling Lebreu that he was Deputy US Marshal Fannin and showing him his badge, he handcuffed him and started on the long way back to Fort Smith.

Three days later, as they neared Fort Smith, the pair had to wait by a railroad track as a train went by. Fannin's horse shied as the train rumbled past, so he dismounted, and as he did so, Lebreu made a break for it, grabbing the reins of Fannin's horseAs he started to gallop away, Deputy US Marshal Fannin pulled out his pistol and shot Lebreu in the back, killing him. Fannin now had a problem: the rule was that the accused had to be brought back to the court alive. If he was dead then the officer could not collect any fees and, if the deceased had no relatives or friends, burying the body became his responsibility. It cost Deputy US Marshal Fannin 60 dollars to bury Jason Lebreu.

What happened to Deputy US Marshal Dave Fannin is not known. The records of all the Deputy US Marshals that were kept at Fort Smith were very scant and one can only assume that Dave Fannin either resigned and moved away, or he just continued to work as a lawman and drifted into obscurity without attracting any more attention.

Chapter 35

Seth Bullock

Seth Bullock was one of those lawmen that never really got the credit he deserved. He was the first elected sheriff of Deadwood when it was a lawless town.

He was born in Amherstburg in Ontario, Canada, in the early 1830s, the son of a retired British sergeant major. His father, a strict disciplinarian, made Seth Bullock's early life almost unbearable, so much so that he ran away from home at the age of 13 and again at 16, this time to live with his sister, Jessie Bullock. At the age of 18 he left Canada and moved to Helena, Montana, where he immersed himself in local politics and the community and unsuccessfully tried to get into the Territorial Legislature.

Undeterred he continued his political work and in 1871 was elected as a Republican to the Territorial Senate and was one of the founder members of Yellowstone National Park.

1873 saw a change in occupation when he was elected sheriff of Lewis and Clark County, Montana. He immediately set to work enforcing law and order, showing no fear or favour to anyone. One incident that demonstrated he was not afraid to face up to the task of keeping the peace was when he faced a mob during a hanging. A horse thief, by the name of Clell Watson, had been caught by Seth Bullock in the process of stealing a horse. Watson immediately pulled out his pistol and fired at Seth Bullock, hitting him in the shoulder. Despite being wounded, Seth Bullock managed to subdue Watson

Head and shoulders shot of Seth Bullock.

and arrest him. Horse stealing carried the death penalty in most parts of the West at the time and as Clell Watson was about to be hanged, a mob suddenly appeared, scaring off the hangman. Without a moment's hesitation Seth Bullock climbed the scaffold and pulled the lever that sent Watson to his death. He then held off the mob with his shotgun, warning them that he was prepared to shoot anyone who tried to interfere with the law. The mob retreated, realising that he was serious.

Some weeks later Seth Bullock made the acquaintance of Sol Starr, who had been the personal secretary to the governor of Montana. The two men became friends and in August 1876, after hearing of the gold strike in the Black Hills in the Dakota Territory they, decided to open up a much-needed hardware store in Deadwood. The two men purchased a plot of land in Deadwood and set up a large tent/shop with the name of 'Star and Bullock, Auctioneers and Commission Merchants' over the front. They later built a large wooden building on the plot.

The Starr and Bullock hardware store, Deadwood, South Dakota.

Above left: Sol Starr, Seth Bullock's long-time business partner.

Above right: Jack McCall.

Deadwood at the time was a completely lawless town, highlighted by the murder of Wild Bill Hickok by Jack McCall the day after Seth Bullock and Sol Starr arrived. Hickok had been sitting in a saloon playing poker when McCall came in, casually walked up behind Hickok and shot him in the back of the head. A hastily convened court of miners accepted McCall's plea of self-defence, found him not guilty of murder and released him. With lawlessness on the increase Seth Bullock put his name forward for sheriff, and, knowing his background, the local townspeople willingly accepted him. Deadwood had its first elected sheriff.

Seth Bullock got to work immediately and deputised a number of residents. One of his first duties was to confront Wyatt Earp, who at the time was a deputy town marshal in Dodge City and interested in the sheriff's position in Deadwood, to inform him that his services were not needed. Wyatt Earp left to return to Dodge City the following day. It soon became clear to the people of Deadwood that Bullock was a man to be taken seriously and who would stick to the letter of the law. One of the major problems that Seth Bullock faced was the proprietor of the Gem Theatre, Al Swearengen, who had most of the town council on his payroll. Swearengen's theatre was in fact a brothel and a most successful and lucrative one, earning Swearengen tens of thousands of dollars a week. He invested a lot of the money in businesses within

The Gem Theatre, Deadwood, South Dakota.

Deadwood, which cultivated alliances from the more powerful and wealthy of the town. Seth Bullock had a number of run-ins with him during the time he was sheriff, but was unable to bring him to justice.

With the situation in Deadwood being carefully controlled, Seth Bullock sent for his wife Martha and daughter Margaret from Michigan, where they had been living with her parents until he had got everything settled. They later had another daughter, Florence, and a son, Stanley.

A chance encounter with Theodore Roosevelt in 1884 was to be a turning point in Seth Bullock's life. He was in the process of bringing a horse thief by the name of Crazy Steve into Deadwood for trial when he met Roosevelt, who at the time was the deputy sheriff of Medora, North Dakota. The two shared coffee and a meal on the tailgate of Roosevelt's wagon and quickly became friends. This friendship was to flourish throughout Seth Bullock's lifetime.

In 1881 Seth Bullock and Sol Starr had purchased a ranch at the point where Redwater Creek met the Belle Fourche River, calling it the S&B Ranch, just three miles west of the town of Minnesela. With the railroad making inroads across the West, Seth Bullock and Sol Starr persuaded the Fremont, Elkhorn and Missouri Valley Railroad to extend their

215

Above left: An excellent shot of an unknown sheriff on his horse, about to ride out.

Above right: An older-looking Seth Bullock.

railroad across some of the ranch land that they owned. Within weeks of the railroad arriving, Seth Bullock and Sol Starr had founded the town of Belle Fourche, with the offer to businesses in Minnesela of free lots to build on. It didn't take long before the town of Minnesola began to look like a ghost town and the new town of Belle Fourche flourished. It was later to become the county seat. As more and more trains began arriving, Belle Fourche became the biggest livestock-shipping centre in the United States. The two partners also invested in a flouring mill and in mining with investments in the towns of Spearfish, Custer and Sturgis.

In 1894, a fire ravaged part of Deadwood and Seth Bullock's hardware store and warehouse was destroyed. Seth Bullock and Sol Starr decided to build a hotel on the site of the original store and warehouse. The Bullock Hotel took two years to complete at a cost of $40,000. It had three floors and 64 rooms with a bathroom on each floor. It quickly became the focal point of the state and was the most desirable luxury hotel of its time. This historic hotel is still functioning today and boasts a 24-hour casino.

The Bullock Hotel, Deadwood, South Dakota, built by Seth Bullock.

With the outbreak of the Spanish-American War in 1898, Seth Bullock volunteered to join Roosevelt's Rough Riders. He was awarded the rank of captain and given command of Troop A, Grigsby's Cowboy Regiment. However, it was a relatively short war and Seth Bullock's outfit sat it out in a Louisiana training camp.

217

Sol Starr and Seth Bullock.

In the meantime, Theodore Roosevelt had gone into politics and in 1905 was elected President of the United States. To celebrate his friend's victory Seth Bullock organised a group of 50 cowboys, including the actor Tom Mix, to ride at the front of his inaugural parade. Later that year Seth Bullock was appointed United States Marshal for South Dakota. Four years later he was reappointed, this time by President Howard Taft.

When Theodore Roosevelt died in January 1919, it came as a bitter blow to Seth Bullock, who had been in close touch with his friend from the first day they had met. With the help of the Society of Black Hills Pioneers he had a monument erected in Roosevelt's honour. Nine months later Seth Bullock died on his ranch near Belle Fourche and was buried in Mount Moriah Cemetery along with Wild Bill Hickok and Calamity Jane.

Chapter 36

Texas Rangers

The story of the Texas Rangers goes back to 1823, when Stephen Austin, known as the father of Texas, recruited 10 men to protect between 600 and 700 settler families who had arrived in Texas after the Mexican War of Independence from Indians. However, the first officially recorded man to be known as a Texas Ranger was in 1835, when Robert McAlpin Williamson was selected to be the first major of the Texas Rangers. Slowly but surely the number of Texas Rangers grew and, following the Texas Revolution in 1836, which created the Republic of Texas, the newly elected president, Sam Houston, increased the force to 56. Two years later Mirabeau B. Lamar took over as President of Texas and almost immediately sent the Rangers to fight the Cherokee and Comanche Indians that had supported the Mexicans in the Cordova Rebellion. The Rangers were soon in action again after a band of Kichai Indians raided Fort Smith, causing some casualties. A party of 18 Texas Rangers was sent to deal with them and became embroiled in a gunfight in which 10 of the Rangers were killed. The remaining eight, having lost their horses and almost all of their equipment, had to walk to the settlement on the Sabine River some considerable distance away.

Sam Houston became President of the Republic once again and immediately increased the force of the Texas Rangers to 150. Texas Rangers badge.

Throughout his tenure as president, the Texas Rangers were involved in skirmishes with the Indians and Mexicans. In the Mexican–American War of 1846, a number of Texas Ranger companies were used by the government in counter-guerrilla operations, using their extensive knowledge and experience of fighting against the Mexicans. This was very apparent in the engagement with the Mexicans in the city of Monterrey, when the Rangers' experience of house-to-house fighting became crucial in the defeat of the Mexican Army. At the end of the war the Rangers were all but disbanded, but in 1857 the Texas Rangers were resurrected when Harton Richard Runnels was elected governor of Texas. He immediately allocated $70,000 to the rebuilding of the force. The Texas Rangers, now under the command of John 'Rip' Ford, started to recruit and within a matter of months Ford had over 100 well-armed Rangers at his disposal. They were almost immediately in action because of raids by various Indian tribes on settlers and their properties; these included the Battle of Little Robe Creek in 1858 against the Comanche and the Battle of Rio Grande City in 1859 between Mexican Cortinistas and regular soldiers, in which the Rangers supported the regulars. The success of the Rangers in various campaigns and skirmishes enhanced their reputation and the US Army came to rely on them for support with the increased Indian raids. Surprisingly, although their effectiveness in controlling the Indian population was widely recognised, the Rangers were once again disbanded just prior to the American Civil War.

With the advent of the American Civil War, loyalty to the south caused a split in the number of Texas Rangers, although the vast majority supported the south. Throughout the war Rangers distinguished themselves, mainly because of their experience in fighting wars, whereas the vast majority of the Confederates were either volunteers or enlisted men, most of whom had never fired a gun in anger. After four years of bloody war, which divided some families irretrievably, the south surrendered to the Union and a period of what was to be known as reconstruction began. In 1870, in order to maintain a semblance of law and order, an organisation similar to the Texas Rangers called the Texas State Police was created by the Union. Three years later it was disbanded and the newly elected Governor Richard Coke and the state legislature immediately recommissioned the Texas Rangers. Over the following years the reputation of the Rangers grew and grew.

In 1872 the newly appointed Sheriff John Clark and Cattle Inspector Dan Hoerster had put together a posse after a tip-off about a gang of cattle rustlers led by the Backus brothers. They intercepted the gang and

A group of Company D Texas Rangers. Standing, from left: Jim King, Bass Outlaw, Riley Boston, Charley Fusselman, Tink Durbin, Ernest Rogers, Charles Barton and Walter Jones. Seated, from left: Bob Bell, Cal Aten, Captain Frank Jones, J. Walter Durbin, Jim Robinson and Frank L. Schmid.

A posse of Texas Rangers resting during a patrol.

221

after a brief fight captured five of them, including the Backus brothers Liege and Pete, together with Charley Johnson, Abe Wiggins and Tom Turley.

On the night of 18 February a large mob, equipped with a battering ram, broke down the door of the gaol, dragged the five men out and took them to the edge of town and prepared to lynch them. In the meantime Sheriff John Clark, together with a visiting Texas Ranger, had managed to get a group of six local townspeople together and pursued the mob to the edge of town where there was a large oak post. They were too late to save the Backus brothers and Abe Wiggins, as they had already been strung up, but they managed to save Tom Turley, while Charley Johnson took the opportunity to make good his escape in the confusion that followed. Over the next year a vigilante committee, known as the Hoodoos, carried out a number of midnight hangings of rustlers and outlaws who fell into their clutches.

These lynchings increased over the next few years, together with a number of shootings of innocent people who objected to the 'Hoodoos' and their methods. This came to a head in 1874 when a prominent American rancher by the name of Tim Williamson was confronted by a gang of men, led by German rancher Peter Bader, and accused of stealing a yearling. After a heated argument Tim Williamson was shot dead by Peter Bader. A grand jury was convened but failed to indict anybody for the murder, and within weeks a spate of revenge killings began. This forced the governor, Richard Coke, to take action and so he ordered Major Jones of the Texas Rangers, together with 40 men, to go and sort the problem out and arrest those responsible. By the end of 1876 all were either dead or imprisoned.

The Rangers were now making their mark in Texas and were becoming one of the most-feared law organisations in the state. Sheriffs, town marshals and US Marshals were now asking for their help in hunting down outlaws, and some of the more notorious ones, like John Wesley Hardin and Sam Bass, were captured by the Texas Rangers. Such was their reputation that the Apaches dreaded the Texas Rangers, as one Apache warrior said, 'When they followed our trail, they slept in the saddle, ate while they rode or went without and their guns were always loaded and their aim unerring'.

In 1877 the Rangers suffered a heavy defeat in the San Elizario Salt War, or the El Paso Salt War, also known as the Salinero Revolt. This was a complex range war with political and legal undertones and revolved around the ownership of the immense salt lakes situated at the base of the Guadalupe Mountains in west Texas. What started out as a legal and political struggle among Texan politicians ended up as an armed struggle by Mexicans and settlers living on both sides of the Rio Grande near El Paso, against politicians William Wallace and Albert Jennings Fountain, who were supported by the Texas Rangers. After a bitter struggle the Texas Rangers, now reduced to just 20 men and under siege in San Elizario, surrendered to an army of over 500 men. The victory was short-lived, as the arrival of the African-American 9th Cavalry and a large sheriff's posse consisting of a large number of mercenaries caused the army to retreat. The end result was that the once community-owned salt lakes were now under private ownership and hundreds of Tejanos (Hispanic residents of Texas) were forced to flee to Mexico.

Texas Rangers Putnam and Philips.

Despite popular belief, not all the Texas Rangers were pillars of society. Many had criminal records, and in some cases they were just as ruthless as the men they were chasing. Some were even known as 'criminals wearing badges'. From a historical viewpoint, the wearing of a badge was synonymous with law and order and the first of the Texas Ranger badges appeared in around 1875, made from a Mexican silver five-peso coin in the shape of a star.

In 1875, the Mason County War suddenly erupted. It was sometimes called the 'Hoodoo War' because of the masked vigilantes who were members of the 'Vigilance Committee'. Disputes between the German immigrants and the Americans had been festering for some time because of increased rustling, with each accusing the other. The result was that there were a number of mob lynchings and retaliatory murders before it was resolved by the actions of the law and the Texas Rangers.

One posse of Rangers, led by Leander McNelly, was among the most ruthless of all the Rangers and was known to have resorted to torture and even mock execution to obtain results.

A lot of stories surrounded the Texas Rangers, some borne out of tall tales, but in the main they were based on truthful incidents, unlike a lot of the stories about outlaws like the James brothers and gunfighters like Wyatt Earp that filled the newspapers or 'penny dreadfuls' at the time.

Handmade silver Texas Ranger badge made from a five peso coin.

The vast majority of Rangers were unmarried, and were not drunkards or braggarts, but decent brave men. Most of the Rangers' reputation was earned between 1858 and 1901, and one of their most famous arrests was that of Billy Thompson in Travis County in 1876, who was wanted for murder. Thompson had been avoiding lawmen for over two years, but he encountered Captain John Sparks of the Texas Rangers, who was leading a small posse of Rangers looking for a rustler by the name of Neal Cain. They were in the act of raiding the Cain ranch when they came into contact with Billy Thompson. John Sparks immediately recognised him and promptly put him under arrest. His brother, Ben Thompson, was told of his brother's arrest, and immediately sought out a lawyer to represent him. Ben Thompson also contacted Arkansas County, in the hope that they would extradite him to stand trial for that murder, rather than being sent to Kansas.

The following year the Texas Rangers were once again called in to help the local sheriff when the Sam Bass gang carried out a series of stagecoach, train and bank robberies, all within a 25 mile radius of Dallas. A special company of Texas Rangers led by Captain Junius Peak was sent to the area and was quickly in pursuit. Sam Bass, who knew the area well, was able to elude the posse with ease, but one of his gang, Jim Murphy, informed on the gang, telling the Rangers about the next bank to be targeted, the Williamson County Bank in Round Rock. He had cut a deal with Major John Jones, commander of the Frontier Battalion, in an effort to save himself from prison.

Armed with the information, Jones dispatched his Rangers to the town of Round Rock where they planned to set up an ambush. On the morning of 19 June 1878, Sam Bass and his gang entered the town for a preliminary look around. Not to raise any suspicion, they entered the local store and purchased some tobacco, but as they were leaving the local sheriff, Caige Grimes, approached them. Thinking that they had been recognised, one of the gang pulled his pistol and shot and killed him. In seconds the street erupted into gunfire from the Texas

Rangers and lawmen. The gang returned fire and then went to their horses and tried to run the gauntlet of shots. Sam Bass was mortally wounded as he rode out, hit by several bullets, as was a deputy sheriff. Sam Bass was found later lying helpless in a field just outside the town. He was arrested and taken to the town gaol where he died the following morning. The remainder of the gang disappeared and were never seen again.

It was a Texas Ranger that prevented the assassination of US President William Taft and President Porfirio Diaz of Mexico during a planned meeting in El Paso, Texas, in 1909. This was the first meeting of the two presidents and one that was to take President Taft into Mexico for the first time. Because of threats of assassination being levelled at both presidents, security was extremely tight, with 4,000 American and Mexican troops, along with US Marshals, Texas Rangers and Secret Service agents tasked with keeping the two presidents safe. The day before the summit was due to start two Rangers, Frederick Burnham and Private Moore, were walking the route when they spotted a man behaving suspiciously by the El Paso Chamber of Commerce. This was at a point where the presidential motorcade would slow down and any assassin would be only be a couple of feet from their target. After watching the man for a few moments they approached him and detained him. On searching him they discovered a palm pistol and he was promptly arrested. The meeting went off without a hitch.

Incidents along the Texas–Mexican border continued to flare up and the Texas Rangers were continually called upon to enforce the law, sometimes with brutal results. One incident in January 1918 raised serious questions about the control being exercised over these posses. After a shooting incident in the small border town of Porvenir, Presidio County, Texas, the Rangers went in to deal with it, with the result that 15 members of the population, ranging in age ranging from 15 to 72, were shot dead. Despite heated protests about the killings, no one was ever charged.

The bandit wars continued along the border, with skirmishes carried out by Carrancistas and Seditionistas, mainly because they were unable to carry out a full-scale attack on Texas, so had reverted to hit-and-run raids. These raids tied up the US Army and Texas Rangers for many years before they finally fizzled out.

It was a Texas Ranger who brought a pair of America's most notorious robbers and criminals, Clyde Barrow and Bonnie Parker, to justice. In

Dead mexican bandits killed at
Battle of norlos Ranch. Tex-Mex-Border.

Above: Dead Mexican bandits being dragged by Texas Rangers after being shot dead during an attempted robbery on the Norlos Ranch on Texas/Mexican border.

Left: Texas Rangers Wood and Saunders.

1934, Captain Frank Hamer was brought in to track down the Barrow gang after they had successfully managed to help one of their gang, Joe Palmer, escape from a prison farm. One of the guards was killed during the escape, which added to the list of killings (nine of which were of law enforcement personnel) that the gang had carried out over the years. The breakthrough came when one of the gang, Henry Methvin, looking for a way out, told the authorities that the gang was going to visit a house in Bienville parish. An ambush was set up at the road junction between Gibstand and Sailes. In order to get Bonnie and Clyde's car to stop, Sheriff Henderson Jordan and his deputies had persuaded Methvin's father, who was known to the gang, to be on the side of the road with his truck.

On the morning of 23 May, after waiting for a couple of days and almost ready to give up, the sound of Clyde Barrow's Ford V-8 car was heard approaching. The car slowed down and stopped when the occupants saw Methvin's truck. At that moment the sheriff and his deputies, along with Texas Ranger Frank Harmer, opened fire with their shotguns, rifles and Thompson machine guns, riddling the car and its occupants with over 150 bullets. The saga of Bonnie and Clyde was over and their lifeless bodies were taken away.

Lawman examining the body of Clyde Barrow after he was shot in his car.

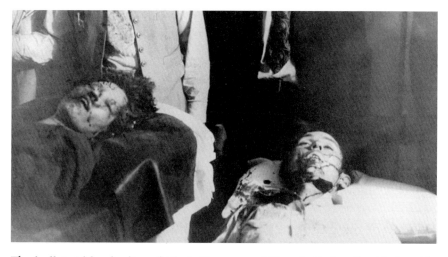

The bullet-ridden bodies of Clyde Barrow and Bonnie Parker lie side by side in the morgue.

The bullet-ridden Ford V8 pilot belonging to Clyde Barrow.

Conclusion

The day of the gunfighter who rode into town instilling fear into the community had passed, as had the scenario in which two men faced each other in the street, waiting to see who was the fastest on the draw. As towns and cities grew, that threat was replaced by fear of organised criminal gangs. As settlements became more civilised and the open carrying of guns was prohibited, a number of federal agencies were created, including the Bureau of Investigation (FBI) and the Border Patrol. The role of the marshal was for a time relegated to that of bailiff and process server, but it was soon realised that the expertise acquired over the previous years was too valuable to be wasted.

The beginning of the 20th century brought a new kind of violence to the West, with immigrants forming their own districts and gangs within cities. In New York, the Sicilian mafia spread their tentacles across the city, while the Irish, Chinese and other nationalities had their own criminal organisations. As other cities grew so did the criminal gangs, and it was the ability of the US Marshals to be able to move from city to city and from state to state, that gave them the power to arrest and detain wherever they were. Today the Russian mafia and South American drug cartels have extended their influence to the United States and have become a serious problem for law enforcement officers throughout the country.

US Marshals, unlike sheriffs, town and city marshals, have the authority to carry out arrests in any part of the United States without a warrant, for any offence against the laws of the United States. They also have the authority to carry firearms anywhere in the United States. Such is their power, that the only person authorised to arrest the President of the United States, is the United States Marshal for the District of Columbia (Washington DC), making that marshal the most powerful law enforcement officer in the United States. The contribution made by the early sheriffs, city marshals and US Marshals paved the way for law and order throughout the United States, and today, despite the excitement that the television and film industry depict for entertainment, it is one of the most law-abiding countries in the world.

Bibliography

Paula Mitchell Marks – And Die in the West. William Morrow & Company, New York, USA 1989 – ISBN 0-8061-28887

Glen Shirley – Law West of Fort Smith. Bison Books, USA 1968.

Leon Claire Metz – The Shooters. Berkley Publishing, USA .1976 – ISBN 978-0-425-15450-2

Eugene Cunningham – Triggernometry. Barnes & Noble. USA. 1996, – ISBN 0-7607-0251–9.

Aft T. Burton – Black Gun, Silver Star. University of Nebraska Press, USA 2006 – ISBN 978-0-8032-1747-8

Index

233